7 Letters to My Daughters

I couldn't put *7 Letters to My Daughters* down! Rani Puranik tells her life-story with vividness and honesty. Her success was built on her ambition and the four D's: Desire, Discipline, Dedication, and Determination, plus the ability to work for long hours every day. No wonder she became a global tycoon in the male-dominated energy business. Impressive. Bravo!

-Barbara Taylor Bradford, OBE
Author of 'A Woman of Substance'
and 39 additional best-selling novels

Rani Puranik illustrates her authenticity, personality, honesty, and courage between the pages of this beautiful book. She addresses big issues with ease and intention, inviting each of us to think deeper, unite, and dissolve the barriers between cultures. Rani lives boldly and bravely and shares her valuable insights of Love, Leadership, and Legacy. *7 Letters to My Daughters* is a wonderful blueprint for living your best life with purpose, and encourages the reader to utilize the undeniable influence on the global human existence we all possess when we simply dedicate and implement our energy for the greater good. This impeccable collection of letters to her daughters is actually a collection of letters addressed to each of us!

-the Honorable Joanne King Herring
American socialite, business woman,
political activist, philanthropist, and author

LIGHT LESSONS OF
LOVE, LEADERSHIP, AND LEGACY

7 LETTERS
TO MY DAUGHTERS

RANI PURANIK

NEW YORK
LONDON • NASHVILLE • MELBOURNE • VANCOUVER

7 Letters to My Daughters

Light Lessons of Love, Leadership, and Legacy

Published in New York, New York, by Morgan James Publishing. Morgan James is a trademark of Morgan James, LLC. www.MorganJamesPublishing.com

Proudly distributed by Publishers Group West®

Scriptures taken from the NEW AMERICAN STANDARD BIBLE, © 1960, 1962, 1963, 1968, 1971, 1982, 1972, 1973, 1977, by The Lockman Foundation. Used by permission.

Quotes from the Tao Te Ching from *Sacred Wisdom: The Tao Te Ching: 81 Verses by Lao Tzú with Introduction and Commentary.* Translated by Ralph Alan Dale, Watkins Media The Limited, 2006.

Morgan James BOGO™

A **FREE** ebook edition is available for you or a friend with the purchase of this print book.

CLEARLY SIGN YOUR NAME ABOVE

Instructions to claim your free ebook edition:
1. Visit MorganJamesBOGO.com
2. Sign your name CLEARLY in the space above
3. Complete the form and submit a photo of this entire page
4. You or your friend can download the ebook to your preferred device

ISBN 9781631958977 paperback
ISBN 9781631958984 ebook
Library of Congress Control Number:
2022932245

Cover Design by:
Melanie Cloth,
Zilker Media

Interior Design by:
Christopher Kirk
www.GFSstudio.com

Morgan James PUBLISHING Builds **with... Habitat for Humanity®** Peninsula and Greater Williamsburg

Morgan James is a proud partner of Habitat for Humanity Peninsula and Greater Williamsburg. Partners in building since 2006.

Get involved today! Visit: www.morgan-james-publishing.com/giving-back

To Bhakti and Sharayu.
There's always a way to be playful, powerful, and purposeful.

TABLE OF CONTENTS

Daughters of Light

November 2020
1:15 p.m., Houston, Texas

How sounds differ
As my daughters take their stride.
Little giggles of shy talks
Blossom to stories of laughter's pride.

Younger wants and needs
Now alter to
Thoughts and considerations,
"What to wear" and "When to play"
Graduate to "Who to meet" and "What to say."

Friends take center stage
In a pool of their choices and dreams.
Mom's guest appearances
Applaud unconditional love
In every scene.

I pray for all daughters
To live as lights of their own
And shine their message
Of why they were born.

Each girl a blessing
In every mother's vision.
Roles may change
From past to future.
Do remember we all are
Daughters for a higher reason.

PREFACE

One beautiful Saturday morning in 2017, my daughters and I were enjoying a simple, delicious, homemade brunch on our patio in Houston, Texas. We laughed as we watched our two dogs, Socks and Beans, play their floppy-but-focused game of tag with a brilliant green dragonfly. The sun beamed "Hello!" and my heart swelled with joy.

I glanced at my two daughters and marveled at the beauty God bestowed within each of them. My elder daughter, Bhakti (which means "devotion of love") has a contagious laugh, an elegant style, and an uncanny sense of adventure. She is creative, thoughtful, and full of strength and wisdom.

My younger daughter, Sharayu (which means "as the wind flows with intention") has an innate fire to seek truth beyond trends and popular belief. Quite the orator, she thinks deeply and has a unique ability to articulate in a moving way. Sharayu smiles big, lives out loud, and when she enters a room, everyone knows she's arrived.

Bhakti glanced around, inhaled deeply, and said, "Ma, you know, we've come a long way."

Sharayu added, "And we're so proud of you, Mom."

I smiled and shied away. "For what, my beautifuls?" As a woman and mother, it's easy to get lost in overdrive. For extended periods of time, you can become trapped in the motion of getting it done. Fully committed to nurturing, growing, investing, connecting, and oh, yes, achieving. Then, every so often, a moment of clarity and a ray of light become present, sometimes through song, a conversation, something you watch or experience. You realize all the things you've learned, how much you've grown, sacrificed, shared, faced, overcome, succeeded in, or endured. This was one of those moments.

We began a trip down memory lane. Reminiscing about times of triumph and disappointment and exchanging stories of humor, fear, anxiety, exhaustion, and surprise. We belly-laughed hard and we shed many tears. Gratitude expanded within, and in an instant, my eyes opened to what I previously couldn't see.

I've waded through waters that tested and buoyed me and sometimes threatened to take me under. A learning moment of betterment was available each and every time. Of course, I could choose to be aware of it, or I could choose to ignore it. However, if I chose to ignore it, the same lesson would chase me—no, hunt me down—time and again until I addressed it, which was oftentimes quite painful. For years, I could not understand why certain lessons persistently vied for my attention.

I assumed next-level achievement or progress always meant easier with less stress and struggles. Later, I realized life is a continuous journey of ups and downs, wanes and waxes, tests and tribulations. We go through seasons, phases, and levels much more complex than the basic Pac-Man arcade game I grew up playing in the 1980s, Mario Bros. in the 1990s, or Candy Crush of today. In the game of life, we get to the next level by increasing our skills, recognizing the patterns, learning strategies to maneuver through challenges, and never giving up.

Lessons learned at each level build both our armor and character. In addition, I've learned things can become easier over time due to a combination of two things: awareness and love. Holding on to them is the key to endurance and improvement. They open our minds and hearts, and serve as reminders that there is always a way to be positive, playful, powerful, and purposeful while overcoming challenges.

I have come to realize that each day gets better with an awareness of who I am and a connection to all that is around me. Each day holds the opportunity for growth and transformation when we choose love.

As we picked up our dishes, wrapping up breakfast, I mumbled in passing, "Maybe I should write a book."

I heard the sound of a fork falling to the ground. My "clean up" instinct kicked in, and I turned to retrieve it, only to see Sharayu frozen, eyes locked with her sister's. In unison, they screamed, "Yes, you should!" immediately followed by an outburst of happy dances, as if they knew what was to come.

Bhakti raised her glass of orange juice to toast. And just like that, my beautifuls lit a fire within me that day to share the lessons I've learned of life, love, leadership, and wisdom. I embarked on this journey with the intent of creating a gift for my daughters and all daughters of the world, one that provides lessons to equip them to maneuver through the phases of life.

Popular science tells us that the cells in our body are replenished every seven years. After each period of renewal, we literally become a new person from the inside to the outside. Of course, the actual science is a little more complex than that, but I've always been drawn to the idea that we evolve at regular intervals. I'm living proof of it.

After some introspection, I realized my life, when divided into seven-year eras, was defined by unique identities, some of which I chose willingly, and others of which were chosen for me. Yet, each was a new exploration of my life, and each posed its own questions for me. Now I faced new questions. *What does it mean to be a daughter, a sister, a lady, a wife? How can I convey my evolution and life lessons in a meaningful way?* My fondness for letters paved the way for my decision to write one letter for every seven years of my life and compile them in book form.

As days and years passed, a variety of delays, from the most tragic to the seemingly trivial, came to pass. I now realize the power in doing all you can, when you can, and in trusting the timing of things you can't control. These misfortunes and missteps allowed a final letter to be written, providing the conclusion for all seven chapters.

Pieces of your path may not always come together in the way you desire, but they will make a way. With love and awareness, every puzzle piece lays the groundwork for forward movement.

Now, finally, my seven letters are complete, and I am gifting them to you, my dearest daughters.

Introduction

THE POWER OF SEVEN TIMES SEVEN

was twelve years old, full of excitement, running out of our very Indian home in Houston, Texas. Laser-focused, I darted toward the mailbox, which was perched at the curb on a pole, like a New York City skyscraper owning the block. My *aaji*, which means grandmother, had written me another letter in our native language, Marathi. To the best of my ability, I had finally finished my response. With a sense of accomplishment and endearment, I proudly raised the red flag so the mail carrier would know I had a letter to send to Thane, India.

Writing and receiving letters has always brought me joy, even from my earliest childhood years. The intimate and warm connection conveyed from handwritten correspondence is unmatched by other forms of communication. Although it can't contain emojis and memes, nor can it be instantaneously edited, captioned, or forwarded, a letter carries the heartfelt gift of time and intention set aside with the receiver in mind.

In some ways, I find a letter even more meaningful than an in-person conversation. As a child, when I received a letter, I couldn't help but imagine the other person writing to me in response. The writer takes a few moments out of their day to sit down, carefully choosing the pen, ink color, and paper style to physically write the letter, pondering which words to use, pausing between sentences, and sighing a gentle exhale as memories cause a tickle or a tear. Handwriting is a reflection of care, legible and neat, as the writer thinks hard about the best way to communicate.

When I decided I was ready to share my story and the lessons I have been fortunate to learn on my life journey, I knew it would have to take the form of letters. I wanted the medium to reflect the message, something personal and direct, prepared with care.

As I write this, I am in a unique position. Since many of my phases are complete, I can pause to reflect.

Did I say pause? That's so unlike me. All I've known my entire life was to do and keep doing. I was always on a quest for happiness, to figure out the meaning of love, to race against myself and find ways to see differently, while shying away from my true self. Along the way, I discovered how to lead amid uncertainty. I dug to uncover my spirit. I dared to see myself as I truly am in the mirror. I strived to know my purpose, awkwardly but assertively proclaiming my faith, and yes, bravely yet humbly surrendering to God.

I've spent so much of my life searching for identity and meaning, that I've seldom had the space to pause and think about what has come before. A friend once said, "Revati, you've come a long way." I didn't quite know how to process that. There were so many more challenges to overcome and lessons to learn and so much more to do to fulfill my purpose and destiny.

As a Hindu, I come from an unquestionable understanding of karma, the belief that our destiny is based on our actions and interactions with the world. My belief includes reincarnation, which is the rebirth of souls into new bodies and lifetimes. The ultimate key to freedom, moksha, is the understanding of what is truly real and the liberation from rebirth. As such, I was determined to do whatever I needed to be one with the universe and end the cycle of rebirth. Who, in their consciousness, would choose to be part of this mess on Earth? I, for one, wouldn't. Therefore, I wanted to quickly learn every lesson so I could move on and attain moksha.

Let's just say God sure has a sense of humor. My world changed when I learned I was already free. With one heartfelt prayer, I could break away from this cycle of karma through unconditional love and acceptance of myself and my journey. I could create my own destiny through my actions, interactions, and goals. I could forge my own way, one step and one day at a time. Still, I have come to realize that even while I practice self-love and appreciation for others as part of the universal whole, the world treats me very distinctly as female.

It's funny how I now see myself as compared to how others see me. When I finally opened my aperture—widening the camera lens to let the light shine through—I was able to see everything clearly and in the way it is supposed to be seen. Life is meant to be lived in a panoramic view.

Many years into my career, in a meeting at the office, a newly hired young lady turned to me and said, "I'm so honored to work for a woman CFO. I really look up to you and would love to understand what you do and how you got here."

A bit shy when receiving praise, I replied, "Oh, it's nothing, really. I'm sure you can do it too." I then explained what I do, and while pointing to different countries of the globe, I paused. I realized that, in fact, *I had* come a long way. For years, I had crisscrossed the globe for personal and professional reasons, and leveled up time and again to evolve personally, emotionally, and spiritually. My life has always been more than just a series of moments. It was all part of a larger pattern: my seven-year cycles.

With every second, every breath, and every circumstance, we are all evolving. Looking back, I can see how my life was distinctly designed to take on specific roles as a *female* every seven years, but the lessons of love, leadership, and living free were truly about what it means to become a *person* in this world.

This book is about the human experience. I give a voice to the person I have been. Being a woman, in particular, has nuanced the landscape upon which my circumstances arose, but my emotions, struggles, fears, faith, and attitude through the pain and joy are what any human being might experience. Parts of my life have been challenging, and they may come across as frightening, painful, or deeply sad. I do not flinch from sorrow or suffering or the jaw-dropping, unbelievable moments of victory. Some of my experiences will be very familiar, particularly to women, but also to anyone who has struggled with belonging, both in the world and in personal relationships. This may bring up distressing memories for you, but I urge you to continue reading.

Every person has a backstory. We are all towering flames kindled by our most formative years—our childhoods. Every passing season, every experience, every interaction serves as firewood which, when lit, becomes the fuel to our passions, desires, and relationships as our lives continue. It is this light that can drive away the darkness of self-doubt and fear. It is also this fire that may drive away growth, love, and confidence. It informs the choices we make, both conscious and unconscious.

I believe even the most arduous parts of my life have brought me blessings. My request is that you read these stories with a positive light because, to the best of my ability, that is how I endured and continued to move forward through it all.

Now, with years of distance and perspective, I recognize how even the lowest points of my life had value and guided me toward something greater. I promise you, the ending to this story, and yours, is happier than you can imagine.

Chapter One:

WHEN I BECAME A GIRL
BIRTH TO AGE SEVEN

Step into the unknown, for herein lies your destiny.
~ Unknown

What a tremendous gift it is to be born. For many, the upcoming birth of a child is the beginning of celebrating a life full of mysteries. No matter your cultural background or where you are from, the range of emotions experienced—anxiety, joy, or outright fear of the unknown—is universal. Planned or unplanned, boy or girl, from the first sound of the heartbeat to the first kick in the belly, we wait with bated breath for the tiny stranger inside to emerge with a cry to let us know "I am here."

Both my parents grew up in India. They came from traditional, lower-middle-class families with no life experience outside of their limited world. They met while playing badminton. Mom was twenty and Dad was twenty-six. Although they didn't meet through an arranged marriage, they certainly didn't know each other well. In a most unconventional manner, my mom asked my dad to marry her shortly after they met. So the newly engaged couple had one short year to get to know each other before marriage.

In June 1970, Dad received a full scholarship to Louisiana State University and left in August to settle in, followed by Mom in January 1971. They adhered to the accepted way of living based on their heritage and tradition. Their hearts and minds were very much Indian, which meant they were spiritually and fiscally conservative. They always worried about the future and were self-reliant, never borrowing money.

My parents never thought of themselves as poor. Quite the opposite, they saw the resources they had as opportunities for a better life. Dad earned a student stipend while obtaining his master's degree at LSU, and Mom sold Avon. They aimed to live on ten percent of what they earned and sent the remainder back home to their families in India.

Sometimes, events that appear to be unfortunate are truly blessings in disguise. A car accident during my mother's eighth month of pregnancy with me was one of those blessings. In March 1972, my parents and a group of friends were returning to Baton Rouge from Galveston, Texas. Suddenly, my dad slammed on his brakes to avoid colliding into an existing accident chain on the freeway. However, the car trailing them couldn't do the same and slammed into our car. The driver came over, profusely apologizing to my dad, and even more so to my mom when he saw her very pregnant and petite self in shock. Immediately, he handed her $2,000, a handsome amount back in those days, to show his remorse for the situation. My parents graciously accepted the offering, and they all went their separate ways.

The amount was enough to cover a flight for my mom to return to India where she could be with her mother, in the comfort of a familiar environment, for the birth of her first child. Unfortunately, Dad was not able to join her because he had to relocate to Houston and prepare for his new job as a metallurgist. This was a pivotal shift in my destiny. In a crash second, I was destined to enter the world in India rather than the United States. Being a citizen of India by birth caused some of my most challenging obstacles. If I had been born anywhere in the United States, my stories would be drastically different.

In 1972 in Thane, India—a tiny town just outside of Mumbai—there were limited medical services and interventions available. There were no epidurals, and rarely an obstetrician. Having her first child here was my mother's preference. She had been living with my father for two years in the United States in Baton Rouge, Louisiana, when I was conceived. After learning she was pregnant, she immediately knew she wanted to have her baby in a place that represented familiarity and safety. She was to be a mother for the first time and wanted to be with her family, in a place she understood, where the aroma of spices enveloped the thick, hot air, the sitar and tambura always echoed in the distance, and the language dripped easily off her tongue.

On the day of my birth, as my mother lay in the strange physical and emotional twilight that follows the delivery of a human being, her midwife approached with a grim face. "I'm sorry," she said, "but it's a girl." Thus, I entered the world as an apology.

It's probably for the best that we don't retain memories of the actual process of being born. They would be intense, if not traumatic. Instead, most of us hear about our birth through the prism of the memories our parents choose to share. The circumstances of my birth and what it meant, not just for me, but also for the burgeoning family I was joining, are enshrined within the story my mother has told me several times.

Across the many cultures of India, boys are more highly valued than girls. This is especially true when it comes to the firstborn. A firstborn takes on the name and legacy of the family, protects and provides for the parents in their old age, and furthers the family's goals and reputation. My father was a firstborn. He'd done his best to live up to all those responsibilities. He was no doubt looking forward to the imminent birth of his first child, a son.

For my father, having been raised with very clear ideas about the prescribed roles of men and women, a firstborn daughter was almost like having no children at all. Who would take on the leadership role after him? Who would be his right hand as he aged? Who would ensure the continued future of his family? For my mother, a very young woman at twenty-one years old, she felt she has been unable to give her husband what he desired.

I don't know how she told him or what my father said in response when we arrived in Houston. My mother never told me that part of the story, but I do know that throughout my childhood I was very conscious of the realities surrounding my birth and my very existence that twisted together like thick, thorny vines.

I was a girl. And I was a disappointment.

My Mother, My World

"Sunnnn-ny dayyys, sweeping up (big inhale here) clouds awayyyy. On my wayyy to where the air is sweet . . ." Mom often joined me as I sang the *Sesame Street* theme song. It helped us both learn English. The song eventually took on a greater meaning, becoming an ongoing affirmation for me and a way of life. My mom spoke the lyrics as she settled into life in the U.S. in support of my father as he built a company from scratch. I sang the words as a reflection of my ever-cheery spirit, that is, before I began engaging with others outside of our home.

When my parents came to the United States, my dad didn't mind being slightly progressive. He appreciated westernized clothing, tried new cuisines, was curious to learn about trends in science, and always thought out of the box when challenged. That's how his mind worked. On the other hand, my mother was very traditional. She adhered to the normal Indian working-class ways of existing, including the belief that Hindu scripture should be read every day. She was terrified of losing her roots and values in America, and she didn't have the education, language proficiency, or experience my father had, which made adapting to life in a new country that much more difficult.

Like my mother and father, I stood out. I didn't wear American clothes. I didn't have blonde hair or white skin. I didn't know the games they played, the celebrities they loved, or the TV shows they watched. At the time, I didn't speak English yet, apart from that theme song to *Sesame Street*.

I was raised sheltered, without casual meetups with other kids or the excitement of playdates, as our household was led primarily by the mother's mindset. I was told to mind my own business and not think too far ahead since, according to Mom, we would go back to India soon. I was not allowed to listen to the radio except for the one Indian channel that played for a couple hours on Saturday. The only other access to the outside world or entertainment was the Public TV station with educational entertainment and sprinkles of occasional family shows like *Little House on the Prairie* or *The Waltons*. With very little exposure to life outside our home, I don't remember ever worrying about what was going on in the world. My family was my world.

Mom taught me to read by the time I was four, and she took me to the library religiously. I checked out any book I could get my hands on, even those aimed at older kids. My hunger for learning didn't stop at reading. Math felt very natural to me, and I could do addition in my head early on, which I later learned was a skill I shared with my father. By the time I was enrolled in kindergarten, I was so far beyond grade level that I was quickly bumped up to second grade. I excelled in intellectual pursuits because I spent so much time inside my haven, in my own head.

Baba (my father) tells me the story often of when he and my mother dropped me off at daycare when I was about two and a half years old. This is also a flash memory for me. I remember how painful it was to watch them drive away, tears streaming down my face, and wondering if they would ever return. It was sheer trauma for me. Baba told me that this scene ached his heart as well.

Rarely did I feel lonely, even when I was alone, but the times I did feel a sense of loneliness were invariably when I was surrounded by other children. I was different, so the children mostly avoided me. In my solitude, I experienced some of the benefits of being born a girl. The freedom of expression to sing and dance at will encouraged me to pursue those passions. My love of moving my body led me to study ballet and other forms of dance, as well as gymnastics. Had I been born the longed-for son within my family, my parents never would have allowed me to explore those interests.

I had an entire world of my own that didn't require anyone else. I was extremely creative, and found ways to be happy, even mischievous, when things got too serious. I eagerly gravitated toward the outdoors, swinging and monkeying around on the parallel bars. At other times, I could be found in my creative space in my room. The beauty of this world was that I could take it anywhere. I needed no props, no assistance, and no input from adults. I was never bored, and despite my isolation, almost never unhappy.

Perhaps because of our culture, or simply due to our family dynamics, we were not a very affectionate family. Most of the love I got was tough love. Appreciation was hard to come by. The words, "I love you" were not part of the culture, and minor bruises or cuts were met with, "No need to complain, be strong, wash it off, and go back to play."

My mom was also a huge proponent of hard work and discipline. She believed we all had to go through hardships to be rewarded in life, and she reminded me of this even as I fell off to sleep. Instead of hearing the sweet sound of lullabies, I drifted off to her voice singing a classic Marathi song: *"Arey saunsar saunsar, adhi hatala chatake, tewha melatey bhakar."* My mother sang, "Oh, life, dear life, only when my hands learn from the burn of the stove will I get my bread to eat." This beloved

Marathi song became a foundational philosophy of 'my fire pit' and represented a solid life lesson that prepared me for the future.

My internal monitoring of my conduct and performance grew into a deep fixation. My goal was to be perfect, whatever that meant. During the first week of second grade, the teacher gave us a list of ten rules to follow. They were simple: "I will not speak out of turn," "I will be respectful toward my friends," and so on. She told us if we broke the rules, we would have to sit in the corner and write all ten of them ten times.

As soon as she said that I set feverishly to work. With the perfect penmanship of a young scribe, my masterpiece punishment task was ready for presentation in advance. When the class took its first break of the day, I went up to my teacher and handed her ten neatly written copies of the list.

"But, Revati," she said, bewildered, "You didn't do anything wrong."

"Yes, but just in case I do, now you have this," I told her, with all the gravity a six-year-old could muster.

A Grandmother's Praise

My maternal grandmother, Leela Date (for me, my *aaji*) a tiny yet mighty woman in her own right, was the first in my family to identify and nurture the qualities in me that would eventually guide my character and my life. She saw me as strong above all else, strong in mind and body. She encouraged me in dance, and especially in gymnastics, even though girls of her generation hadn't engaged in those pursuits.

Instead of chastising me to be still, quiet and reserved, she praised my boundless energy and told me to jump as high as I wanted and to run as fast as I could. Not once did she try to replace my exuberance with traditionally feminine virtues like grace and obedience. Never did she request that I be more docile. As far as she was concerned, God had blessed me with a strong and flexible body, and I should make full use of that blessing.

She would visit us from India for six months or more at a time. As her first grandchild, she and I developed a special relationship. She taught me to read and write in Marathi. She told me stories that broadened my imagination. Through her loving observation, she was one of the few people who focused on my positive attributes and affirmed me. My grandmother saw things in me long before I did, almost from the time I was born. Even when I was being punished by my mother (in our household, like many traditional Indian households, punishment was usually corporal), my grandmother would point out how I refused to cry or scream. Instead, I laughed and tried not to show any fear.

"Look at her!" My grandmother would say. "She is a force!"

Just as excited as I was waiting for the arrival of her special letters, I was even more excited awaiting her arrival. I'd make sure everything was in place for her comfort and for our adventures. With the precision of an event planner, I sneakily made plans for activities that would keep her mostly to myself because her praise momentarily filled the void I felt as a result of my father's emotional distance.

Her approval was like a healing balm to me. She provided my earliest lessons in what a girl could be. From her, I learned a girl was not just an inferior version of a boy. A girl could be strong. She could be smart. She could endure. She could persevere. She could be stubborn. And it could all be praiseworthy.

Early in my life, my family started calling me *Rani*, which means "Queen" in Marathi and Hindi. It's a very common nickname for little girls, much like calling a girl "Princess" in America. My grandmother, however, always called me *Rana*, which means king. Specifically, she called me *Rana Pratap*, which means "Victorious King" and comes from the name of a legendary Rajput ruler. I believe it was her way of giving both a benediction and a prediction. "*This* is your first-born son," she told my father. She was letting me know at a young age that I was meant to be a girl, and a powerful one at that. While crossing through the living room to the kitchen, I could never just walk across, that was too boring. So I always did cartwheels all the way through. After hearing my aaji say those words to my father, well, let's say I gained at least twice as much energy!

When I was a child, all I wanted was to be a better daughter, a perfect daughter. But my family, including my beloved aaji, held fast to the tradition of the firstborn being a son. Therefore, many of my experiences prepared me to walk in that role, whether I liked it or not.

Dearest Daughters,

If I could speak to your adorable cuteness at this age before seven years, I would make a basket of songs and poems describing all your goodness! I love the way you glimpse at your tiny toes, not even knowing they are made for taking large strides. Your eyes open wide as your hands first discover sand and water. You embrace everything with such curiosity and love, totally unaware that you are made for game-changing play in this world.

My beautifuls, my heart. Your tiny hands, your precious feet. I see how you love. You give without holding back. Your laughter rings light to the whole world. Your nod has a wonder and an adorable curiosity. I love when you are surprised. You pause as if diving into deep thought and then quickly smile and make me smile too. It is one of your greatest strengths.

From your first babbles and giggles you learned how to say your name. Oh you love your name. I wish I could record your proud and loving expressive response each time anyone asks you to say your name. You show your spunk, your care, and your simple innocence.

I sometimes hold a few minutes on repeat in my mind when I carry you around and we sing together on the park swings. Your smile brightens as you ride in the front basket of my bicycle. Do you know this is where you learned how to fly? Remember the breeze, how it kissed your cheeks and played with your hair? All of that is love my dear. Unconditional, always present love. It's all around you and always there for you.

You already know the secrets to living playfully, with purpose and power. I learn so much from you each day and I pray you never forget your power as you grow in this world. Somehow, you will be tested and not even know that is what it is called, a test. These tests are there to help you learn lessons since they will prepare you for what is to come. Lessons are not to harm you, my dear; they are to strengthen you. I know you will want to pout and ask why you need to be strong. Well, as time goes on, I won't always be there to protect you or pave the way. So, in the most positive and creative way, try to understand these tests as small steps to your freedom, to your happiness. I can't wait to see the way you blossom!

Love always,
Rani

Chapter Two:
WHEN I BECAME A SISTER
SEVEN TO FOURTEEN YEARS OLD

Control is a mirage.
If you walk towards it, it starts to disappear.
~ Unknown

For most people, their first cultural or social group is their family. For me, it was myself and my private world. If the first seven years of my life were defined by my aloneness, the second seven years were all about the company I kept, specifically, my younger sister and brother.

No one told me when my mother became pregnant with my sister, although I eventually realized something was changing in the household. My mother began to look different. She was tired more often. My grandmother came for one of her long stays. I didn't realize it at the time, but she was there to help my mother through the birth. Something was definitely happening, but I didn't know exactly what, and I had no idea how my life was about to change, how *I* was about to change.

The Lucky One

Six years is a significant age gap between myself and the next child, my sister, Shubhangi. The time between children allowed my parents to grow, change, and consider how they wanted to raise their children. It was also a lot of time for me to develop my understanding of life as an only child. I wouldn't understand the heavy implications of this until many years later.

My mother was twenty-one when I was born in India. By the time my sister came along, my parents were still relative newcomers to America, but they had acquired some perspective into the ways of this new country without abandoning their Indian traditions. They had learned some insights about parenting that helped them welcome my sister six years after my birth and my brother two years after that.

My mother wasn't blind to the hurt my father's disappointment in my gender caused me. When she realized she was going to have a second child, she became proactive and enlisted her obstetrician's support. The three of them sat down together and had what was almost a miniature therapy session. The doctor told my father he was going to have a child; it might be a boy or it might be a girl, but either way he had to love his children. The doctor made my father promise he would love the child no matter what, and my dad took that promise seriously.

During this time, many things started to change. My grandmother came to assist my mom through her pregnancy, and I distinctly remember moving from a small apartment to an idyllic house-lined suburb where Mom was especially excited to lay down a beautiful green carpet. My father had become successful enough to buy an elegant golden Mercedes Benz. Lots of changes were on the horizon.

When my sister was born, my parents named her Shubhangi, which means "lucky" or "auspicious one," and my father seemed to have no trouble connecting with her and loving her immediately. He was delighted by my sister and doted on her constantly. Admittedly, that attention sparked tremendous resentment in me. The time I spent trying to please my father, thinking about what he wanted and what I should do and be to make him happy, seemed to evaporate amid the new life that had come into our family. Here was this little creature, totally helpless, seemingly useless, who had effortlessly captured my father's heart. The rejection I felt was undeniable. All my efforts to be worthy of his attention and affection weren't good enough. It felt profoundly unfair.

Of course, my perspective was limited by my age and inexperience. I had no way of knowing, for example, that my father's business was finally starting to take off around the time Shubhangi was born, which had a significant impact on his general mood.

It stung to be stuck on the sidelines as my parents welcomed another child. Our Saturday morning trip to Shipley's Donuts was like a ritual. My sister and I would sway back and forth in Baba's new car as he gleefully whistled some Marathi song. Meanwhile, my mom jokingly complained she had heard it a thousand times already. Then, in the midst of the laughter and fun they both would turn to each other and say, "You know, Shubhangi is such a cute child, so adorable. She has brought so much love into our household," or "Ever since she was born, there's been no turning back."

Despite the unfairness I felt from those kinds of comments, I enjoyed playing with Shubhangi. On those Saturdays we would enjoy our donuts, go to the park, meet up with more Marathi families. The adults became my *maushis* and *kakas* (aunties and uncles). Together with their kids, Shubhagi and I would imagine cool stories and play all sorts of games. At home, she used to stand on my feet as I bounced her up and down, and she would giggle the entire time. I would stare into her eyes and know I loved her, but there was a constant question I tried to answer through my limited understanding of our world: "What does lucky mean, and what does she have that makes her lucky?" To me, it seemed that she had singlehandedly made my parents *want* to be parents. They decided to learn, adapt, and accept their roles as parents to another child in the six years since I'd been born, and she was considered lucky.

I had spent my earliest childhood constructing an insular world for myself where I had full control over everything that happened. I couldn't be rejected or ignored by anyone there because I always got to choose whom to let in. Suddenly, there was an interloper. She was new and different, and she didn't go home at the end of the day. She interrupted my quiet time and put her little hands all over my personal things. She innocently forced me to acknowledge her by her sheer presence, and if I didn't involve her in my play, I would get in trouble. By her very existence, life became more unpredictable in our household.

I wasn't sure how to be a sister, or whether I even liked the prospect. Becoming a sister meant fundamentally restructuring my internal world to make space for someone else. Part of me felt unprepared and unwilling to make such adjustments, particularly for this tiny person who represented a chasm between my father and me. But in a very short time, something changed within me. I realized something profound. I loved her. I loved playing with Shubhangi as she grew, and I wanted to show her my world, even if it meant opening myself up in a way that was not always comfortable. She was lucky, and I was lucky to have her in my life.

A Crush on Krishna

Every woman can remember her first crush. For some, it was the boy next door, and for others, it was a famous pop star with cool hair. Not for me. When I was seven years old, I fell in love with Krishna. It was the kind of obsessive love only little girls and religious fanatics experience. For me, Krishna was my entire world. I read and hoarded everything I could find about him, an illustration here, a book there, gathering them in a place of honor in my room. In the solitude of my childhood and in an attempt, which I now realize in hindsight, to force order into an unexplainable and scarily vast world, I created my own narrative, a steadfast connection to my spirituality that nothing could surpass. Even at such a tender age, I had an unwavering desire to understand and be known by a higher power, a being that could facilitate my strength, love, joy, and happiness.

For Krishna, I would go into the garden each day to collect flowers I would later use to create a new garland to put on my makeshift shrine as I sang made-up songs about him. I kept my worship of Krishna to myself, safely ensconced in my secluded world. It was an exceedingly private, personal thing that seemed unfathomable to share. Even though I had set up my shrine in the bedroom I shared with my little sister, my relationship with Krishna was just that, mine.

For a long time, I wondered why I was so drawn to Krishna. Why him and not Brahma or Lakshmi or any of the other significant figures in Hinduism? An observer would assume it was a childhood fantasy, an aesthetic choice, or just the pure randomness seven-year-olds are prone to. However, I see now that my affinity for Krishna was even simpler than that. I loved Krishna because Krishna understood love.

There are many powerful and important figures in the Hindu pantheon. I knew all the stories about great deeds and divine struggles. Of them all, Krishna was the only one who delighted in simply being. Krishna wasn't about fighting or cursing people. He just wanted to hang out with the cattle and the sheep and play his flute. Krishna knew how to have fun. He lived a free life by simply living. At this time, I didn't know what that meant, but it spoke to me. I learned the full meaning of this much later in my seventh phase. When things got tough, I sought ways to be playful, joyful.

Of course, my Krishna crush couldn't go unnoticed forever, especially after I started wearing a repurposed nightgown and going barefoot all the time in imitation of Saint Meera, who had an unconditional, undying love for Krishna. It all came to a head one day when my mother told me several times to get dressed because we were going out to dinner. Still in my nightgown and robe and still shoeless, I tearfully insisted I *was* dressed. She marched me to my bedroom to get proper clothes. That's when she discovered my shrine.

"What is this?" she demanded. I stared up at her mutely. How could I explain to her what I felt about Krishna, why he was so important to me, when I couldn't even articulate it to myself? Fear rushed from the bottom of my soles, up my legs, to meet my quivering stomach. I could tell she was getting frustrated with me, and that was almost always expressed in one way, with a smack. Sure enough, she waited just a few more moments for me to explain myself, and when I could not, she grabbed me. "You'd better snap out of this!" she said, delivering a few angry blows. "Get dressed and put on your shoes. And take this down," she added, gesturing toward the sticks of incense I had carefully arranged around my limp flower garland.

I don't think my mother specifically objected to worshiping Krishna, or even to worshiping in general (though she objected to me leaving the house in a nightgown with no shoes on). I think she was confused, and she didn't like being confused, especially when it appeared her seven-year-old daughter was deliberately withholding information from her. I realize now that her anger was not so much about what I was doing as it was about her own inability to understand what I was doing. Nevertheless, I interpreted her anger as a demand that I no longer adore Krishna so intensely. I obeyed her, at least, as far as she knew.

Lovesick, I dismantled my shrine. I put away my books and photos and threw away the fresh garland I had made that very morning. My heart was sinking, yet I did as I was told. The demolition of my Krishna shrine could be compared to a teenager being put on punishment and having their phone privileges taken away when smitten with their first boyfriend. The sting of unfair restriction pulsed through me like shackles restraining my freedom. I put on my normal clothes. I wore shoes. I went to the restaurant with my family. However, I didn't love Krishna any less.

What I learned was that I had to hide all expressions of devotion, particularly from my parents. Instead, I turned those feelings inward and kept them for myself, making them more intense. After that, I didn't just worship Krishna at a little shrine in the corner of my bedroom; I worshipped him in everything I did. When I sang, I changed the words to be about him. When I danced and played, I thought of him and how he delighted in those same activities. I built a new, grander shrine in the privacy of my own mind.

Over time, I felt less intensely connected to Krishna, but I was still very interested in the idea of a higher power. I remained drawn to love and joy, feeling more certain that there was a Creator. I felt equally sure he, she, or they had an intimate understanding of love. With that, I began to question the rituals and orthodoxy of religion, specifically the ones I was still expected to observe. Thankfully, although I didn't know it then, my love and adoration for Krishna prepared me for the next shift about to happen in our home.

Our Little King Arrives

The birth of my brother, Mahesh, was yet another seismic shift in our family, one so big even my two-year-old sister recognized it. My parents loved my sister differently than they loved me, but the adoration they exhibited for my brother was an entirely different level of admiration. I was accepted, my sister was loved and considered the pretty one, but my brother was enthroned.

It was August 15, 1980 and our house was filled to the brim with close family and friends as we watched Hurricane Alan sow destruction through our television screen. We were all huddled together in the living room, my very pregnant mother sitting on the sofa with maushis and kakus on either side and my father pacing back and forth on the vibrant green carpet. As the rain and wind tore through the city, my father expressed his concern for how he would get my mother to the hospital if she went into labor. He even preemptively ordered a helicopter service to be on standby that would be authorized to land in our backyard if the need arose.

To eight-year-old me, this was a level of excitement and panic with care I had never experienced; I had never seen Baba so worked up and anxious, and he didn't even know the sex of the baby yet. Looking back, the obstetrician's advice to "love the child no matter what" really stuck with him! Now it was about safety, not about a gender of a child.

When Mom went into labor, the panic in the room increased tenfold. There was no need for the helicopter, however, and they left that night for the hospital. I was told later that it was a complex labor; the baby was breach and Mom was required to have a C-section. After all the external commotion and internal anticipation, my parents finally welcomed their first boy, Mahesh, into the world.

When I visited Mom and my new baby brother, I was amazed and joyfully in awe by the sheer number of flowers, gifts, notecards, and chocolates all over the room. Everything looked so thoughtful and beautiful. But somewhere under my smile and jubilee, I couldn't help but notice and hear the same phrase over and over again: "Baby boy!" "Congratulations on your baby boy!" "Lovely baby boy!" Baby boy, baby boy, baby boy—everywhere. *Finally, they had a boy. Finally.*

At last, here was the son my parents had waited and prayed for. I was loved, and Shubhangi was auspicious, but Mahesh was a seismic shift in our family. My mother and father flooded him with affection. My mother dressed him in tiny versions of royal raiment and told him stories of triumphant Indian rulers of the past. This quickly became another situation in which I had to navigate two different hierarchies in which I played two different roles. I liked to play and take care of

Mahesh. Though my mom depended on me to look out for him as the oldest sister, his tiny self was the king in the making.

The rules Shubhangi and I had to abide by didn't seem to fully apply to Mahesh. If we were judged by a conduct card from school, Mahesh was not. If he got in trouble, it was because his teacher did not understand or consider his creativity and intelligence. In my attempts to parent him as I had Shubhangi—as any elder sister would—I was overruled by my suddenly softhearted parents. Of course, that made it virtually impossible for me to have any sort of authority or say over my brother. The situation was akin to a lowly peasant feeling responsible for keeping a king safe, and yet having absolutely no authority to tell the king what to do, even if he is only a child.

I know now that it wasn't my job to manage my brother in that way. But my desire to be of use and my parents' genuine need for help combined to frequently place me in that position. As we grew into adulthood, that continued as a persistent conflict in my relationships with my siblings. Often, I struggled to not jump in and meddle when one of them made a wrong turn.

By the time Mahesh was born, I began to act in a way that aligned with the title of eldest. My version of a big sister was something between a friend (a playmate) and a parent (a teacher and disciplinarian). I thought of myself as the leader of the pack, and I felt a sense of responsibility toward my brother and sister. Yes, I secretly wanted to boss them around, but at the heart of it all, I had empathy for my siblings and felt the need to protect them. I somehow missed out on sibling fun or confiding in each other to grow through silly stories between the three of us. I was as loyal to them as I was to my parents, which was a tough and confusing position to be in.

In many ways, that responsibility was real. My parents' marriage had never been especially good, and it got steadily worse with each passing year and each additional child. My mother found herself stretched thin with three children, running the accounting department for Dad's business, and a myriad of volunteer and social commitments she had. She relied upon me to fill the gaps in childcare. I read and sang to my brother and sister, and I took them on outings. I played with them and made sure they stopped to eat lunch. I made rules for them and tried to enforce them, doing my best to explain to them what it meant to be a child both in our family and in the wider world outside our home.

I had a reflexive urge to give them things I felt had been lacking in my own early life, specifically expressions of love and joy. Since I didn't have models of what that looked like at home, I learned from other people around me. My mother made one friend who was very open and affectionate with her children, giving them lots of hugs and praise. I admired that, and I tried my best to do that for my siblings.

At the same time, I wanted to shield them from the unpleasantness at the heart of our household. Our parents weren't happy together, and that unhappiness bubbled up into almost every interaction we had. My mother, especially, struggled to control her temper. I often took the blame for some of my siblings' misbehavior just to spare them her wrath. During punishments, I would smile and laugh because I didn't want my sister and brother to be afraid for me or afraid of my mother. I masked my own pain in order to spare them from having any.

Whenever I could, I tried to point my sister and brother toward joy and goodness. They accompanied me to places I thought were beautiful so they would have fun, positive experiences. I made up songs for them and recorded tapes of us singing. We made forts in the trees in front of our house and held picnics there. Our parents did none of these things with me, nor did they teach me to do them; these actions just came naturally to me.

One day, while shopping at Kmart, Shubhangi lingered over a display of blue jeans. They were cute, similar to the clothing my sister's classmates wore. When she looked at me plaintively, I automatically slipped into my role as surrogate mother and encouraged her to try them on. Almost immediately, our mother stepped in and shut the experiment down. While pants were okay, she refused to let us wear blue jeans because they were worn by cowboys who slaughtered cows. Hindus saw cows as holy, so in my mother's eyes, jeans were evil, a detail that had slipped my mind in the store. I had gotten so used to managing my sister, to making the decisions about what she could and couldn't do, I had virtually forgotten the house rules my parents established.

My experience as a big sister was full of moments when I was reminded of the in-between position I occupied. Responsibility without authority is like a passenger train. The train must keep the passengers safe, but it has no say in how the conductor will steer it on the tracks. When I played with my siblings, I couldn't be entirely carefree because in my mind, they depended on me for protection and guidance. But in reality, I was just a big sister, not a mother. I didn't get to set the rules and at any moment, my decisions could be overturned by either parent.

Dearest Daughters,

So many questions and so few answers. I know, it feels like a flurry of people are suddenly coming in and showing you where you belong. It's so easy to follow along thinking you don't have a say.

My dear, love sometimes looks funky and strange, but it's all there. And I so love the way you feel everyone's heart. That's called empathy. You have it and you inspire every person around you, even though you don't realize it. I know you are too young to fully understand the depths of empathy, but just keep it amongst your many questions, so one day the answer will come to you. This will become one of your greatest strengths as you discern and make decisions.

The way you welcome friends or gently step back warms my heart, my dear. In your own way, you are stepping into leading; leading you. Choosing you with others in mind. That is leadership. When you step into leadership you gain experience on how to move ahead within certain constraints. I am so proud of the beauty with which you flow from one situation to another. You do it respectfully, with kindness and empathetically.

You learned quickly that leading is not controlling but allowing. Allow yourself to be truthful. Allow yourself to choose. I know, it feels squishy and uncertain in the middle. And you didn't even ask for it.

My love, as you always have done, lead your thoughts in a positive way even when you feel others don't understand you. Love sticks around. Even when it feels like it has floated off somewhere, it is gathering more of itself so it can come back to you larger and greater! You'll see my dear. Love has a kind of loyalty, it has so many places it can be, but because of who you are, it chooses you over and over again. It always will.

Love always,
Rani

Chapter Three:

WHEN I BECAME A YOUNG LADY
FOURTEEN TO TWENTY-ONE YEARS OLD

The music is not in the notes, but in the silence between.
~ Wolfgang Amadeus Mozart

My interest in faith and spirituality matured as I did, and as I entered my teenage years, I found myself constantly asking my increasingly exasperated mother, "Why, why, why?" and questioning nearly every cultural observance. My logical, fact-seeking, and rule-following brain wanted answers and a full understanding of our cultural beliefs and practices. I wanted to know the reasons behind what we did and did not do, and what it truly meant to be Hindu.

"Why do I have to celebrate Diwali?"

"Why are we praying to Ganesh? Does it matter if we do it a different way?"

"Why do we light candles like that?"

"Why are we saying these verses?"

The answer, almost always, was "Because I said so." Like the obedient child I was, I did as I was told.

Hinduism was the spiritual wallpaper of my early life, and although my family was observant, we were not especially devout. We gave our offerings, we said our prayers, and we participated in all the holy days and celebrations. Yet, for all the presence the gods had in our home, our family didn't talk in depth about our religion. So I was generally left to work out my own relationship to the spiritual world, and that's exactly what I did.

However, I didn't stop asking questions.

Finally, in 1987, toward the end of my eighth-grade year, worn down by my constant need for answers, my mother asked me a question of her own. "Rani, what do you want?" This time, she was genuinely asking, and I had an answer right away.

"I want to go to India." I wanted to learn more about the religion and culture I was being raised in but didn't understand. In America, no one did the things we did. We were outsiders. I was curious about my Indian background and wanted to learn what it meant to be Indian.

My mother agreed to send me to India. Perhaps her decision was out of respect for my cultural yearnings.

When I went to India, I was essentially traveling to a foreign land, although it was the land of my birth. My arrival was both a visit and a homecoming, one that would reveal more about my life than I realized. There is a wonderful, frightening, precarious thing about becoming a lady that encompasses being both girl and woman, vulnerable and capable, eager and uncertain. To be a lady is to occupy the space in between, the chasm between childhood and womanhood that comes after puberty and ends in the early twenties. I would land in India as I entered this space.

With plans to live in India for my ninth-grade year, I had a choice between a Catholic convent school and a Hindu school that integrated social service into its curriculum. The relatively westernized convent school was all female, and all the classes were taught in English. All the wealthy families in the area sent their daughters there, and quite naturally, the school attracted a lot of expats and Westerners. If I went there, I would encounter a number of other Americans, whereas at the Hindu school, I would be one of a kind.

The second option, a school rooted in Hindu faith and practices, was designed to help young people take on leadership roles and become assets to their communities. It didn't have the social cachet the Catholic school did, but it did have a stellar reputation as a top academic school. The only problem was the school was predominantly Hindi-lead, and while some classes were available in English, most weren't. I didn't speak Hindi. I spoke Marathi. I could muddle through a little, based on what I'd gleaned from the Hindi Bollywood movies my family watched like clockwork every Friday and Saturday night, but I certainly wasn't fluent, and I wasn't sure I'd be able to keep up academically.

My personality never allowed me to take the easy route. Challenges were a part of my existence from the beginning. To encounter one more was expected. Of course, I chose the Hindu school. The song my mother sang to me in place of a lullaby was a guiding philosophy. *Oh, life, dear life, only when my hands learn from the burn of the stove will I get my bread to eat.* However, my attitude was never as grim as those words. Always chirpy, creative, and happy, I was inherently playful and full of mischief, so when met with a challenge, my eyes would brighten, and I would take a curious approach. *Hmm, how can I make this fun? What will I encounter this time?*

I wasn't going to India for an American high school experience; I wanted to learn something new. I wanted to understand. The best way to do that was to throw myself headfirst into the deep end, Hindi and all. So I headed for Pune, India, at fourteen years old, to live with my maternal uncle and learn about things I didn't understand in a language I couldn't understand. Fun times! My grandmother lived in a different city and would visit me occasionally. She approved of my choice in schools and proudly boasted to others, "Look at my Rana Pratap. She is a force!" My heart swelled with her love, *Oh, Aaji*.

My sheer excitement suspended any fears I might have felt at the thought of failing a class, not making friends, or being in any sort of physical danger in this strange land. Even when homesickness reared its head, it lasted only a moment and then vanished like ripples atop clear waters. As a child, a girl, a fledgling, just beginning to learn lessons of flight with her newly discovered wings, I saw myself as quite capable and independent. In many ways, that was true.

It was in India that people began to treat me as something other than the child I had been in America, beginning with my schooling. It was a rocky start. My status as an Indian American made me neither fish nor fowl in the eyes of my new classmates. I didn't speak their language fluently or come from their city. I wasn't quite as much of an object of fascination as a white Westerner might have been. Mostly, they thought of me as spoiled. Weren't all American kids? Being treated in this arm's-distance way wasn't new to me. After all, kids in America had treated me pretty much the same way, just for the opposite reason. Instead of being sad about not fitting in, I immersed myself in the experience of school, determined to learn what it meant to be Indian, focused on speaking Marathi, my native tongue, and committed to understanding the disciplined culture of respect.

In school, three classes were taught in Hindi: history, geography, and civics. The school board allowed me to write my exam papers in English, but all the textbooks were in Hindi. Thankfully, I was able to source a translated version of the textbooks, which helped me greatly. As long as I could write my answers in English, all was fine.

I enjoyed the spiritual atmosphere at the school. It was there that I was first introduced to meditation and yoga. I did not know it then, but learning to center myself would carry me throughout the tough years of my life. The first time I closed my eyes and followed the guided instructions, my mind connected with my body. The experience of meditating was new to me, but it felt natural and became an integral part of my lifestyle. I began to see a more explicit connection between my need for a loving God and service to others.

Creative Thinking Saves the Day

At the end of the first semester of my freshman year, I participated in a service project to support rural women who were protesting alcohol abuse among men and the physical abuse that so often accompanied it. We all were passionate about the cause. I worked with a group of mostly women trying to raise awareness of the growing problem of alcohol abuse in rural India. We were specifically working to block the development of a popular pub fueling alcoholism and draining money from the community.

That December, we went on a camping field trip to Khed Shivapur, just outside the city limits of Pune. On our two-hour bus ride, I was still seen as the outsider and sat quietly as I observed forty girls singing our school anthem of endurance and overcoming obstacles. These lyrics were new to me but had a nice groove, so my feet tapped along.

We arrived in the middle of nowhere and unloaded. Breathtaking mountains formed a circumference around the area. The ground was mostly barren, but patches of dry grass grew in various spots. I looked up at a mesmerizing clear sky without a single power line. High above tiny black dots swooped down to become large flocks of black birds and sparrows. In the distance were an open fire, white tents, and a few people setting up. This was our site.

This village was known for training workers to serve the industries expanding in surrounding areas. However, as the pockets of cottage industries were being built in the nearby villages, local pubs and alcohol breweries began to emerge. Unfortunately, as the workers started earning extra money, they would buy alcohol instead of saving or buying necessary household goods for their families. The production of the moonshine distributed at the local pubs required no sanitation and was often dangerous. This posed a serious threat to the health of the community. So, while this specific village should have been an economic stable ground, it was quickly deteriorating due to alcohol.

As we settled in, the camp leader announced our task for the day. "Girls, we are going to fill those large barrels with water," she said, pointing at three wooden tubs, each one the size of a small outhouse. With no faucets or hand pumps nearby, I wondered where the water would come from and how we were to fill the barrels. As if reading my mind, she pointed to the village drinking well, about a hundred feet away, which was surrounded by several heavy-duty plastic buckets. "Start there," she said. My eyebrows lifted. *Interesting distance.*

The gasps and sighs of the other girls were unmistakable. We'd endured a long bus ride to this small village and would now have to do several hours of manual labor to fill the barrels. We had signed up for this, to serve others, so it had to be done. In a somber, single-file line, resigned to their fate, the girls shuffled slowly toward the buckets. I, on the other hand, observed the scene, trying to grasp the whole situation.

Although there were not enough buckets for each of us, we slowly took what we had and walked to the well to fill each one before turning to haul our load, spilling almost half the water on the way to the barrel. This exercise was tiring, tedious, and worst of all, wasteful of a resource this terrain clearly lacked. By late afternoon, we were exhausted and hadn't even filled one barrel to half. With only a few more hours left before the sun disappeared behind the mountains, I wondered how we could do this better and faster? I then recalled a memory from years earlier that brought forth the exact solution I needed for this situation.

One late night at home in Houston, as I climbed the stairs to get to bed, I noticed random items on the floor at the foot of the landing, and more at the top of the stairs. I didn't pay much mind to them, but I knew cleaning up would be on my list of things to do the next morning. As I went downstairs the following morning, my mom asked if I'd brought the things placed at the top of the stairs with me. I didn't know I was supposed to, so I hadn't.

Then she explained, "Rani, *hatasarshi kama karachi asathat. Nahitar, zhada sarakhe te kam vadhat zata.*" "Rani, work through things in one step, on the way, as you go. If you don't, the same job will grow like a tree." If you had been aware," she continued, "you could have brought whatever you could carry in one go. You would have saved time, even created it." That flashback was my "aha" moment.

As we stood around the well waiting for the empty buckets to be returned by the girls who had hauled water to the barrels, I tapped one girl on the shoulder and said, "What if we make a single line from the well to the barrel. One could fill the bucket, then hand it to the others down the line one by one. This way, none of us has to walk the trail, and we won't waste any water."

The instant reply I got from her was baffling. "You may do things like that in America, but we don't do it that way here."

Huh? Why did it matter where I was from? I'd merely suggested a way to make our task easier and more efficient. Despite her judgment, I decided to demonstrate the idea, for the sake of us all. *Oh boy, this may not be easy, but hey, bring on the challenge!* With my water-filled bucket in hand, I stopped a girl midway, extended my bucket to her, and said, "Hi! How about you take this back to the barrel? You're halfway there. Just turn back so you don't have to walk the whole distance."

She was so heat struck and exhausted from the walk, without much thought, she quickly agreed. I took her empty bucket and ran to the well for a refill. On the way back, I stopped another girl from this unnecessary hardship and asked, "Would you please take this?"

She snapped back. "You can take it yourself. I just finished that long walk."

Rolling my eyes, I thought, *Maybe I should give up, do my bit, and watch the redundancy.* But I knew we could do better than a half-baked job. I patiently said, "Yes, you're right, but this way you won't have to do the whole thing again by yourself."

That got her attention. "What do you mean?" she asked.

I answered, "You can take a shortcut and take the bucket from here. It's closer to the barrel." The words "shortcut" and "not by yourself" became key selling points.

Finally, I had my second recruit and the line started to develop. I ran toward the well repeatedly until the distance to run back shortened to a couple of feet. My peers soon formed a human chain. Each carried a full bucket for a few feet to hand it to the next in exchange for an empty one. We started cheering. Claps created a fun beat as all forty girls joined in the connection and the line moved faster. Now it was a game. As water was pulled from the well on one end of the line, simultaneously on the other end it was being poured into a barrel.

What could have taken a full two hours took us less than forty-five minutes. We had conquered the distance and the painstaking effort as a team. To celebrate, we high-fived, did a happy dance, and broke into a victory song. We had used resources wisely and efficiently. We "one-stepped" the task and created time. This was a leadership lesson for me in the power of creative thinking and teamwork. I didn't need to receive any special credit for sharing the idea; I just needed to share it. Others couldn't see the vision I had in my mind until I shared it. And I couldn't bring the vision to fruition on my own. I needed their cooperation.

Our strength, capacity, and momentum increased when we united and turned an idea into action. Steering the idea didn't attract consensus immediately. To materialize it, I had to be humble, patient, and kind, allowing the others to become receptive to and comfortable with a new process. Leading by example is the synchronization of thought, action, and unity. That single lesson has served me well throughout my life.

A Natural Leader Emerges

After my fellow students and I settled in together, we gathered and walked arm in arm with local women and elders from the affected villages to the newest distillery. Our main goal was to tear it down so the alcohol abuse would stop.

Our instructor blew the whistle and one hundred fifty of us, with banners and slogans ready, marched over the mountain and into the village. As we entered, many women sat next to their small, modest huts, watching, unsure what to think of us, likely intimidated by the mass of schoolchildren. I wanted the village women to join us, but they were hesitant. Most of them had a child on one hip and another on their back. My heart wanted to connect with them, so I started speaking to them in Marathi, their native language.

As I approached one woman after another, I held their hands and looked into their eyes, saying, "Come, come, come!" I later learned that was something no other visitors to the village had ever done. Those women and their families were considered untouchable, the lowest level of a historical caste system that, to this day, remains woven distinctly throughout Indian culture and politics.

I never cared about caste or creed or any of those rules. If anything, the caste system disgusted me, and I sought ways to bridge this behavior that amounted to discrimination. So, in stride with my moral compass, I encouraged the women. "Don't be afraid. I've got you. C'mon, we can do this together." I wasn't marching for the sake of marching. I was marching for justice to be carried out.

One woman hesitated at the doorway to her home, telling me if her husband knew she was part of this march, he would beat her up. Standing strong in my fourteen-year-old convictions that women and children are never to be harmed, I told her with an assertive and loving smile, "We are with you, and we are going to do this together." I meant it with every fiber in my being. That was the first time I felt God's presence and peace. I didn't have much context to understand the depth of what was really going on in this community or in her home. All I knew was that I wanted her and every woman in that village, along with their children, to come with me. I knew that, together, we could make a difference.

She stared at me unblinking for a moment. Sensing her fear, I asked her, "Is it okay if I take your child?"

She said, "You can take my child, but I am not coming with you."

"Okay, I will take your child, and maybe you could just hold my hand. I promise you I will not let go of your hand. Then, will you come with me?" I asked.

After a long pause, she said, "I will come, but you have no idea what is going to happen later on."

"We will talk to your husband," I assured her.

She looked at me with her beautiful brown eyes full of fear, and asked, almost in a child's voice, "Do you promise?"

"I promise," I said.

I took her hand, and she waved over her sisters and cousins to join us. Together, we started toward the distillery. As we walked, other kids shouted, "We want to go too!" Our group sang songs and chanted victory cheers as we marched, gathering more women and children along the way.

Finally, I saw a raggedy shack with a white tarp, like a tent, held down by wire and rope. Next to this makeshift distillery stood a group of men telling us that we could not tear it down. I was worried there would be a conflict, but I stood tall, still holding hands with the woman. Then, three very strong and respected women stepped forward, dressed in their traditional Indian saris with large bindis on their forehead. They spoke to the men, powerfully demanding what they needed, what they wanted for their families, and reminding the men of their priorities. One woman's voice soared over the group: "You have got to go and work and put the money back to the family!"

Suddenly, a woman walked up and tugged on the tent. I wanted to be a part of this, so I followed her. Within moments, a group of women and children had surrounded the distillery, pushing and pulling until we brought the whole thing down. Here I was, a teen, being what my grandmother said I was, a force. But this time, I was not alone. I had a strong team of Indian women standing beside me, in my native country, defending other women against a problem threatening their families. I was helping another woman be brave, and she trusted me. She held my hand, which was a source of strength for her. It was a defining moment of my life. I was becoming.

When we arrived back at the woman's home, her dismayed husband stood before us. With a calm voice, I said, "Namaste *Kaka*. You might be wondering why we are doing this. *Kaka*, please, I hope you can understand. Your village is getting good work at the factories, and your families have a good future. I am asking you, like my father, please stop. You have so much more to give. You are so smart. I know you love your children. If I was your daughter, I know you would love me, and I know you would forgive me for tearing this down." He stared at me, showing no emotion, so I continued. "Your wife is scared. She thinks you are going to hurt her." As I spoke, the woman was still holding my hand, squeezing tighter and tighter as I pleaded with her husband, probably expecting the worst.

Instead, he looked into my eyes and started crying. He joined his hands in a namaskar and, with an earnest voice, said, "Little daughter, I don't know where you came from, but I understand what you are saying." He looked at his wife, who glanced down at our clasped hands, and continued. "I will not hurt her, I promise, and I swear by you I will never drink again."

The woman raised her tear-filled gaze, slowly transitioning from fear to relief to joy. I looked into her eyes and for the final time said, "It's okay," and released her hand gently. She stood there as her husband came close to her and stood by her side. I smiled and gave her a hug, an uncommon gesture among villagers. To my surprise, she hugged me back, and then she took her children and stood with her husband together as a family. She and her husband joined hands in a quiet and calm namaste. Our eyes met for the final time. I didn't know if this was a form of love, or God, but whatever it was, I was grateful.

That act of service and kindness, creating and seeking genuine interactions, caused others, including my teachers, to take notice of me. Actively wanting to communicate with people and be part of a team went a long way in that school environment, focused as it was on training people to be mindful of others and to work for the benefit of the larger community. By not seeking the approval of others, and merely acting from the kindness within my heart, I had inadvertently become someone who was different in a good way, instead of in a weird way.

For the first time in my life, I had an abundance of friends. At first, the attention was bewildering, yet I quickly grew to cherish these new relationships, making sure to open the door to anyone who wanted to know me. At the time, I didn't know what leadership skills were. I was just being me, and that was enough to form meaningful connections with other girls. After the march, instructors saw the leader I had previously kept guarded. The other girls suddenly wanted to hang out, to sing, talk, and even sit next to me on the bus ride home. It transformed how I saw myself. Before, I had been willing to strike out and do my own thing without wondering if anyone would follow. From then on, I saw that my interests and my way of being could actually be a connector between me and others. I didn't have to be wealthy or have the right clothes or know all the inside jokes. It didn't matter that I was an American transfer student who had to learn the language. I had value just by virtue of being myself.

Days later, our school principal joined us in the common gathering hall, where we assembled each morning to recite scripture and listen to announcements. His presence there indicated to us that something special was about to take place, since he only came for special events.

He stood in front of the hall and addressed us all. "I am happy to share that we have a special award to present today. A student showed a level of leadership at camp we have not seen and is much appreciated. Her unique ideas and exemplary skills united our girls in activities and made a remarkable impact on the villagers."

I looked around the room. *Who could he be talking about?* Then, I heard whispers around me and saw everyone looking in my direction. "It's going to be you, Revati," one of the girls declared. I shrugged my shoulders, smiled shyly, and nodded. *Could it be me?* Then, it happened.

"Revati, please come to the front and accept your award."

The entire room echoed my name with a thunder of claps. I froze, but then, a girl sitting behind me tapped my shoulder and nudged me to get up and go toward the front. As I walked slowly, gazing downward, a happy smile crept across my face. I accepted my certificate and beautiful gold *diya*, an oil lamp. I was speechless, grateful for the recognition. As proud as I was to receive the acknowledgment, nothing compared to the joy I had in my final namaste to the village family I said goodbye to. That experience taught me awards are cool, but my joy was in making a positive impact.

Just as I was finally feeling a sense of acceptance among my peers, I knew I would not remain in Pune much longer. After one school year, I returned to my family home in Houston, Texas, to enter a special business administration magnet program for my sophomore year at Lamar High School.

In many ways, coming back to the US was like pushing the reset button. Once again, I was the weirdo, the one on the outside looking in. This time, however, I never found the magic key that unlocked the approval of my peers. They made fun of my clothes, my hair, my face, everything about me, and they weren't shy about it either. None of that mattered this time because once I began to see myself more clearly, I started to explore other forms of self-expression, particularly singing.

From the age of six, singing was an intimate passion for me. Early on, I was drawn to classical Indian singing, based on the science of notes and their compositions called *ragas*. Performing it properly requires practice and focus on technique and vocal control. As a child, I would sit in my room and listen to performances and try to reproduce them. Once I decided to learn a song, I would practice obsessively for hours until I could hit the notes just right. This was my version of the typical American teenager holding a hairbrush like an imaginary microphone and singing in the bathroom mirror until they are performance ready. My grandmother would call me to dinner, and even though I had been singing the entire afternoon, I would beg her to wait so I could do it again, "just one more time."

This was my form of fun, but also a way of nourishing myself. It was a kind of spiritual practice in a time when I didn't feel comfortable expressing my religious feelings openly, even among my family. Inviting other people to share in this creative expression of singing bolstered my confidence in feeling accepted and appreciated.

By my last year of high school, I practiced four to six hours every day. Our house had a small turret, and after school I would take my harmonium up there and sing my heart out. There were nights when I would be up late doing my homework, and still, I would wake up at 4:00 a.m. to practice my morning *ragas*. Singing never felt like work to me; it felt like home. It was my comfort place, my worship space, and a time when I could be with myself and not wonder if I was too ugly, too weird, or too anything at all. When I was singing, I was just Rani, and that was a perfectly good thing to be.

When I finished high school in 1990, I told my parents I wanted to go back to India and make a real attempt to get musical training. I was diligent and devoted, but there was a limit to how much I could teach myself. At that time, there was no way to get the instruction I needed in the United States. My parents never disapproved of my singing, though they were bemused by how much it obsessed me because they didn't see it as a viable career path for me.

Even though I was a daughter, I was still the firstborn, and my father had already started to see me as someone who could help him with his company, Worldwide Oilfield Machine (WOM). The specialized business administration program I'd taken in high school was chosen to train me to work with him. On top of that, he expected me to take a direction in college that would further prepare me to enter the family business. He was happy to send me to India and allow me to continue my singing, so long as I also took the traditional university route to earning an academic degree.

This was actually one parental expectation that didn't feel so burdensome. Oftentimes, the eldest child in a family with a legacy business feels pressured to follow in their parents' footsteps. Not me. I enjoyed being able to connect with my father over work. It was in the realm of business that my father could finally see me as a leader, a support to him, a positive contributor to the family legacy. My mind worked in a similar way to his. We shared specific knowledge of the business world that no one else in the family had. This was another opportunity through which I hoped to connect on a deeper level with my dad and to be appreciated by him.

I wanted to maintain that connection so much that I enrolled in two colleges, taking two difficult paths of study—business, and my father's major, engineering—so I could follow in his footsteps. Two months into this experiment, I realized I had been characteristically overambitious. In high school, I was able to juggle my responsibilities and my passions, but taking a full load of commerce and engineering courses on top of serious musical instruction proved virtually impossible.

Eventually, I asked my father if I could drop engineering and focus on singing. He agreed. His caveat was that I limit this period of artistic self-exploration to one year and that I complete my college degree afterward. "You must finish school," he admonished me. "That is the most important thing."

I decided to make the most of my year of discovery. I was eighteen years old and once again alone in India. This time I was living in my family's vacation home in Pune. A housekeeper, who was more like family, came by daily to help cook and clean. It was as though I had been plunged into a particularly solitary form of adulthood. I could set my own schedule, make my own decisions, and even run my own household, small as it was.

In Pune, I trusted my instincts and allowed myself to go where my heart led me. I could explore both the city and my interests, so long as I stayed within the parameters my parents had set. More importantly, I was discovering what made me feel fulfilled and purposeful. I was getting closer to my ever-evolving sense of faith and who or what God was.

Nurturing the Desire to Give Back Through Teaching

Each morning, I walked past an impoverished neighborhood, what we call a slum in India. Makeshift homes cluttered the arid landscape, erected with sheets of flimsy tin tied together with hemp rope and covered by roofs lined with torn canvas. Children played in the dusty soil throughout the day. Most of them did not attend school, likely because their families could not afford the cost of uniforms, supplies, or transport to reach the nearest schoolhouse, often more than ten miles away. They would wave and call to me as I walked by. These were the children of the maids, cooks, and gardeners I'd known over the years. Every time I saw them playing aimlessly outside their tiny houses, a gut feeling tugged at me. *This is wrong. They should be in school.*

One day, the younger brother of our housekeeper came with her to work. The boy, about eight years old, settled into a corner of our home, looking determined to tackle whatever assignment his bound papers held. When the housekeeper asked if I could help her little brother with his math homework, something inside of me perked up.

"Of course," I said. "I'd be happy to help."

Together, we patched together his well-worn notebook, assembling the pages in proper order. Each page held dusty graphite remnants from pencil smudges and eraser marks, indicating his determined attempts at completing his lessons. As we began the math problems, I quickly realized that paper and pencil alone were not enough to help this eager boy grasp the calculations. Instead, he needed real-life examples to make the problems relatable to his young mind. I translated each word problem into illustrations he could grasp.

His wide-eyed smile revealed the magical moment of understanding. "I was never taught like that. I get it now."

A spontaneous idea spurred sharply and brightly within me. I could not contain my excitement. *How many more kids like him need this kind of help?*

Knowing I'd need to get permission from the parents and grandparents, I went about the next few days speaking one on one with adults in the slum about helping their children with homework. One day, I approached a grandmother sitting outside her home. She could barely see, but I sat next to her and asked if I could teach the neighborhood children. When I explained I would help them with homework, she immediately consented and so did many others.

I offered impromptu classes, short lessons on basic literacy, numeracy, and cultural instruction. I helped with homework and gave tips on how to study better. And we played. We sang, danced, and had fun. This was my joy, to see the kids lighten up, be free from their stresses, and just be kids and tap into their creative minds. It wasn't anything fancy, but it must have been more attractive to the children than playing at home.

Within two weeks, my makeshift class swelled to sixty local kids, ages five to fifteen. My parents' home was bursting at the seams from the front porch to the washing area in the back. Soon, I realized that children would happily go anywhere and do anything, even homework, if it meant they were seen and given positive attention in a safe space. This was the same kind of nurturing attention my grandmother had given me, and I'd blossomed in her presence. Now, I was giving back in the same way I had lovingly received. My heart was filled with joy.

For two hours each evening, between math and English, we played games, wrote poems and jokes, sang, and practiced expressing values of respect and kindness. We had debates so kids could share and sharpen their views. They were free to speak and express their opinions without retribution, perhaps for the first time for some. There was love and consideration. Each child was making progress.

Coming from some of the most impoverished neighborhoods in Pune, these students had no reliable access to materials or toys. Instead, they had become accustomed to getting their education from an ad hoc system of older kids, occasional brief stints in school, and the kindness of strangers. There was little in the way of media, so their worldview was confined to their familiar neighborhood. The children were desperate to exercise their minds and eager to learn because they had so few opportunities to do what children are built to do: explore and discover.

The more children I recruited, the more thought I put into the curriculum. The students welcomed each new resource. "C'mon," they would say to one another, "let's go to see Rani-tai!" *Tai*, in Marathi, means sister, a term often applied to non-family members to denote a closer relationship or to show respect for an older person.

It was an honor to be called *tai*, the elder sister who knew things and understood the world. I, who had so recently eaten my lunches alone and wondered if any other kids would ever like me, was an authority in their world. It was humbling and a little bewildering, but it also felt very natural to provide a safe space for learning and positive engagement for them. Volunteering my time and energy for others felt sacred, like a form of worship, in a fundamental way. The space the children made in my heart was boundless. Through them, I discovered the power of love and its vast ability to open minds.

After we'd finished the lesson each day, I would take them to the top of a hill that faced my house, and we would talk about life, values, religion, and India. "What was the best part of your day?" I'd ask. That question became as ritualized as a daily prayer, faith, and observance intertwined with human connection. We would chant the Hindu scriptures every evening—by this time, I knew them by heart—and I would ask them to tell me about their lives. For years, my mother pushed and instructed me on Hindu values, but living in India and being with those children made me appreciate the true meaning of the scriptures I once mindlessly memorized out of compulsion. I had discovered a portion of my purpose in life. Soon, however, unforeseen circumstances would shake my world completely.

An In-Visible Threat

During my first summer in India, my mother came to visit me. As any mother would, she had worried about me living alone. When she saw the flock of children I'd collected, she grew concerned.

One morning, while I sat in front of her as she braided my hair, she said, "Rani, what are you doing?" I knew she was talking about my makeshift school, and by her tone, I could tell she didn't approve. Her voice sounded the same way it had when she discovered my shrine to Krishna. Once again, I couldn't quite find the words to explain the calling I felt or how vital it was that I keep doing this.

My simple reply was: "I'm teaching."

"You've got to stop this," she said. "It isn't safe."

Curious at her reaction, I said, "Mom, they're just kids. They only come over for a few hours in the evening. They're not bothering anyone. I didn't start the school to stop it. I'm going to keep going."

My mother stopped braiding my hair and yanked my head at my response. She recognized the time had long passed when she could change my behavior with a few swats. Instead, she insisted on hiring a security guard to watch over the house and me. Her concerns seemed inflated. Despite our family's relative wealth compared to the surrounding area, I didn't think we had anything worth stealing, so I didn't share her fears about burglars and thieves. I always felt safe in our vacation house. However, if a security guard would make my mother breathe easier while she was back in Texas, that was fine by me. It seemed a simple solution for a concern I didn't understand and refused to argue with my mother about.

In India, I was becoming an independent lady, or so I had come to believe. Although I appreciated her concern for my safety, I disagreed with her negative position driven by fear. Unbeknownst to me, however, my mother had identified a danger I didn't even know was lurking. She was afraid not for me as a child, but for me as a young lady. I did not yet know that there was another kind of danger, one that existed for me because of my fundamental nature—my body, my femaleness, even my youth. None of this was said openly.

Sexuality and physicality weren't discussed in our family or culture, and the absence of that discourse left me naive in many ways. I had fabricated my own understanding of romance and sex, mostly from hushed and half-heard anecdotes from my peers, but there was still much I didn't know. For me, sex was like a dark room with only a cracked window for light, enough to see the general contours, but not the details of things. I thought romance and sexuality, and even sexual assault, were reserved for desirable women—pretty girls.

Throughout my youth, I had been told so many times, by boys and girls alike, that my face was ugly, my skin was ugly, my body was ugly that I believed them. Surely, I would never be at risk of falling victim to the predations of men. Who would ever want me? I was acutely aware, even as a child, that my younger sister was the pretty one. This belief was so ingrained in me that whenever a boy showed a casual interest in me, I either completely failed to notice or actively discouraged him, telling him that he should choose someone else.

Once, when I was about fourteen, a boy passed me a note that suggested he liked me and wanted to know if I was interested in him. I was completely nonplussed. I immediately informed him that he'd made a bad decision and should pick some other girl to like. "Or else people will think you're ugly like me," I said. This didn't mean I never had crushes. It just meant I didn't expect them to go anywhere.

Even if I had found someone who reciprocated my feelings, I knew my parents would never allow me to do anything even approaching American-style dating. My parents, like most parents of their age and cultural background, thought in the long-term when it came to relationships. The concept of "seeing someone" without intending to marry them was foreign and frivolous. We all took it for granted that I would one day have a marriage that was, if not actually arranged, at least heavily influenced by my parents' judgments. The idea of marrying without the explicit approval of my parents was unthinkable for me at the time. Still, they almost never pressed the issue.

Marriage was something I was dimly aware of, in the same way a teenager knows they'll one day need to pay taxes or buy insurance. It was a responsibility for my future self to manage. For now, my parents were content to let me find my own path, and they were not eager to see me married. My mother reflected that she herself had been too young to marry at twenty-one. She had not been raised with a clear understanding of sex and sexuality or the ways of being a wife. She wanted me to wait until later in my life to make that decision. My father, of course, prioritized my education. Relationships and weddings were a conversation that could come later.

My life, at that point, was ideal. I had created a makeshift school and loved seeing the children's progress. I was dancing, singing passionately, and learning from a guru. I had a social life and a decent group of friends. I was in college and on track academically to complete my studies and fulfill my father's wishes. For those first three months in India, everything seemed perfect in my world, until it wasn't.

There's no way my mother could have known the man she hired to be my protector would become my predator. I wonder, sometimes, if there were signs I missed, little interactions or behaviors that might have indicated this security officer saw me in a sexual light. In my world of hope and happiness, I was unable to see the present danger, the open pit yawning before me. My mother wanted to keep me safe and shield me from danger, yet even in her best efforts, the danger presented itself.

The security officer hired as my protector held a senior position with the local police. He knew our family in passing, but he had a much closer relationship with a nearby family who were friends of my parents and acted as guardians for me in Pune. They'd recommended him to my mother when she expressed concern about my safety. He was supposed to be safe, not just a good man, but a protector who would stand between me and anyone who threatened to hurt me. All along, he was silently stalking me, gaining my trust while waiting for his moment to strike.

He came by weekly to make sure everything was okay in the house and that I had no troubles. Those visits were usually brief, even perfunctory. The children would be scattered throughout the house, and he would look in the window and wave. He never came inside.

One night, at the end of September 1990, during the festival of Ganesh, he came to check on me after all the children had gone. Outside, people were celebrating. There was a parade with drums and shouting, and it was all very loud. The noise was the perfect cover for his ill intentions. I had just showered and was relaxing in my gown. I'd chosen to stay in and was happy to watch and listen to the crowd from my window.

With a knock on the window from outside, I noticed the security officer wave as he passed by my home, only this time he lingered at the door. "You're here at this time?" I asked from within the house. "My kids have gone."

He said in a deep voice, "It's festival season, and I want to make sure your upstairs is secure. Someone could come through the window into your home. Can I check it out quickly?"

He had never done so before, but the ruckus of the Ganesh festival seemed an appropriate reason for his concern, so I acquiesced, appreciating his diligence. I was in my innocent bubble, unconcerned for my safety, not realizing the threat I had allowed to enter. He relied on my trust, and my guard was down.

As I led the way upstairs, walking the hallway and peeking into each empty room, I felt a hand on my left shoulder, then another on my lower back. Culturally, both in India and as a Hindu, touching another is inappropriate, particularly someone who isn't your spouse. I was stunned, unsure of what to do. I glanced at him quickly, then turned away, trying to write off his indiscretion as an accident.

Then, he said, "Show me the other room." Despite the sudden feeling of warning rising in my gut, I second-guessed myself. Ever the rule-follower, I did as instructed. When I walked to the other room, he saw my pull-up bar attached to the doorframe and asked, "What is that?"

I said, "I do my pull-ups there."

Baiting me, he said, "Really? Can you reach that high?" pointing at the middle of the bar suspended at the top of the doorframe. He took advantage of my naivety to make his move.

"Yeah, sure," I said, baffled by his strange question.

"Show me," he said.

Stepping into the room, I grabbed the bar and pulled myself up, like I'd done a hundred times before. As soon as I clenched the bar with both hands, he stepped closer and grabbed me by my armpits, suspending me in the air, my feet unable to reach the floor.

"Let me go right now!" I said, panicking.

Instead, he pulled my body closer to his, our faces inches from touching. The smell of alcohol burned my nostrils, causing me to squinch my nose. The stench of sweat reeked from his pores, and I felt sick to my stomach.

When I realized what he was trying to do, I screamed and kicked wildly, squirming and struggling to free myself. I stretched my left leg and put my foot on the edge of the mattress, using it as leverage to push away from him. Suddenly, a burning energy sparked within me. It was like the force of a fire igniting in a split second, taking down anything in its path in a dangerous, uncontrollable rage. Like a blaze, the energy moved swiftly and forcefully inside me. *Don't think, don't look back, keep going. Blaze ahead, Rani. Fight, push through, take out anything that gets in your way. Go!*

Releasing the steel bar from my grasp, I landed with both feet on the floor. Like a ninja, I grabbed his right hand in one swift movement and yanked it behind his back. Then, with the strength of an angry bull, I used the full force of my petite body weight to push him down the stairs. He stumbled multiple times, grasping unsuccessfully for the handrail, until we reached the ground floor. With a final thrust of my strength, I pushed him out the door, slammed it shut, and pushed against it to block my attacker from getting back in.

Once he was out, I stood there, numb, staring at the shut door, wondering what had just happened, unable to hear my breath over the sound of my racing heart. My hands trembled and my eyes widened. *Breathe, Rani. Just breathe.* My effort to control my heart rate and shaking hands, to calm the burning energy within me, was a natural reaction to the traumatic moment.

Outside, the festivities celebrating Ganesh continued. The god who brings fortune, provides blessings of abundance, and protects all was being honored while I was being tormented. The drumbeats became louder, the fireworks brighter, the laughter-filled streets busier. All that noise outside obscured a stark reality of deception, the intent of someone who had betrayed a family's trust and perpetrated the most frightening moment I had ever experienced. Perhaps the strength that came over me to fight, to protect myself and throw out the officer with his perverted intentions, was from a higher power. Perhaps it was from Ganesh. My mind was so focused on calming itself from the disgusting act that I didn't have the mental capacity to figure it out in that moment. All I could do was breathe and be quiet, deeply quiet.

In the distance, I heard my housekeeper asking me what happened in a whisper, *"Tai, kai zhala?"*

I kept my gaze on the door and softly said, "I need to call my parents."

She looked at me as I turned toward her, the fear and rage still present in the depths of my eyes. My gaze illustrated to her what she suspected from the noise of the scuffle she had overheard. Woman to woman, victim to victim, she knew.

Getting in touch with my parents was no small act. This was the pre-cell-phone era, and making an international call was a huge production. First, I had to make a booking, which meant leaving a message for the person I wanted to speak to, and then, I had to wait for them to call me back. It took my mother less than an hour to return my call, but it felt like years.

"Rani? Kai ga, kashi ahes?" my mother asked. "Rani? Tell me, dear, how is it going?"

With my pulse racing, my breath shallow, and my thoughts running three thousand miles a second, I spoke quickly and with a slightly raised voice.

"Slow down! I can't understand anything," my mom pleaded.

"Mom, you need to come and get me now!" I said. "Something bad has happened to me. I need to come home."

I explained what happened as best I could, still not really understanding it myself. I told her I wanted to come home right away, although the rational part of me knew that was impossible. I wanted to be a million miles away from this place and this house that had once made me feel independent and self-reliant. In that moment, I no longer felt safe in my own home.

My mom explained that she couldn't come immediately, and yet, from my tone and description, she understood the situation was serious. "Okay," she finally said, "I will call our friends. They will bring you to their home, and they can take care of you until I can get there."

I agreed. As soon as I hung up, I started to sob, and I didn't stop until midnight when the neighbors arrived.

In the midst of my deep sorrow, a vision of the past came to light. A singular, simple memory emerged of something I had done about a month after the security guard began keeping an eye on me and our house. In a gesture of thanks, I had delivered flowers and a thank-you note to the police station to show my gratitude for his service. Now, sitting in a puddle of tears, I wondered if my act of kindness had given him the wrong impression. Had he mistaken my kindness for adoration? Perhaps his behavior that night was spurred by my blind innocence. Maybe it was all my fault.

To carry that kind of guilt was wrong and misguided, but I didn't know that then. That horrible incident actually demonstrated the violent assertion of power of one gender over another that is so often condoned in many cultures. His behavior was an act of force, an intentional demonstration of his perceived entitlement over me and my body. He misused his position of power and the trust of my family to exert his distorted desires. In the moments, days, and months that followed, I grappled with how, or whether, I would ever overcome my feelings of fear and betrayal.

Untitled

August 23, 1990
12:00 p.m., Pune, India

It was the 22nd night
Of the month of worship.
The next day was a test
Where I would do my best.

In a festive mood
A requesting call came by
To look over my life
Since he was passing by.

He was a respected elder
Whom my family knew,
And was asked to "protect" me
The female, with a smile so true.

Being my naive nature
I granted permission.
After all
he was the Deputy Commissioner.

I felt a long stare
From the window
Then heard a knock
In between.
It was he who arrived
At twenty-two, fifteen.

He had just spoken to my mother (over the phone)
Who was pleased with his service,
But when the talk finished
His eyes glistened in such a way
That only a girl would know this dismay.

I tried to ignore that view
Thinking it was my fluke.
Out of conversation
He complimented the house
But was concerned with safety
So implied to see the upper part.

What happened next
I dare not detail,
But generalize I will
Without fail.

He kept coming close
Even though I shrugged,
But before returning down
He spoke about my height.
He picked me up
Where I will not say,
I shouted, "Uncle, let me go!"
But he did it again.

I don't remember how I escaped
But I kicked, squirmed, and fought
Till I pushed him to descend the stairs
My hand grasping his arm . . . he was out.

Numb
I will not proceed
Since my pen cannot complete
This tragic, frightening deed.

An Unexpected Request

When my mother arrived from Houston a week later, she didn't talk to me about the incident. In the days leading to her arrival in India, I'd mentally prepared for the possible reactions she might have, ruminating over her facial expressions, hand gestures, and lectures. I wondered if my overprotective mother, who worried about children being in my house, would scold me for going to India in the first place. Instead, she went about managing the house as if nothing had happened.

I hadn't talked to my father and was uncertain of how my parents would react when they saw me. Unable to bear the many possibilities, I resolved to face their reactions when I returned to the States. More than anything, I just wanted to go home to Houston. I didn't want to be a grown-up anymore, not if this was what being a woman meant.

After much thought, and still no conversation with my mom, I thought I had figured it out. She would quietly whisk me away from India and back to the States. Little did I know that she had another plan altogether. To my surprise, she insisted I not come home, and instead, stay in India indefinitely.

"You need to be married," she told me.

I heard her say the words, but my mind interpreted them as if she had spoken a foreign language. *How would being married help anything at all?*

"It's dangerous for you to be single. There are too many bad men looking at you in *that* way. You need a husband for protection."

Was I hearing her correctly? I'd just been sexually assaulted in my own home—our home—and all I wanted was to feel the love, protection, and support of my parents. In all my wild imaginings, I never conceived they would try to solve the problem by insisting on an arranged marriage.

There it was again. Me, being punished and swept quietly under the rug because I was a woman. The urge to scream arose within me as the pace of my thoughts quickened and my body rippled with fear. The last time she found a man who was supposed to protect me, I had to protect myself from him. All my life, I'd thought of myself as ugly. Now, men were so taken with me that it wasn't safe for me to simply live in the world without a husband? Or was she just trying to prevent the spread of rumors about the attack?

"I just want to go home," I said. "Why can't I go home?" I begged her.

My mother sighed. "Rani, you know how it is between your father and me. It is not good, not good. If you came home now, you would end up taking care of everyone." It was true. Their marriage had been troubled for a long time. Many months before, my mom shared the news of her pregnancy. She asked me if I thought she should keep it. She hoped another baby would save her marriage, so at forty, she decided to continue with the pregnancy. That memory, coupled with her present insistence that I remain in India, revealed a truth I hadn't realized before.

My heart dropped with sadness for both of us. She wasn't sweeping me under the rug; she was trying to protect me the only way she knew how. Her desire was for me to find the happiness for myself that she had seemingly lost long ago. With every effort and resource she had, she'd tried to give me the time and space to enjoy my young adulthood, but now the worst had happened. She wasn't trying to push marriage upon me as a punishment or a confinement. She believed it was the only safe way for me to continue to live as an independent person under the protection of our culture and tradition.

"Rani," she said, "it's time for you to get married. It will be for your own good." My lips felt like heavy blocks of ice. I couldn't move them to utter a syllable as she continued. "We know a good boy who you should meet. He's just a couple years older. He's hardworking and very capable."

Can't you understand? I don't need marriage. I want my life back. I want my voice back. These words begged to escape my mind through my lips, but I dared not disrespect her, so I remained silent.

"Revati, you are so young," she told me. "If your marriage is good, then good. But if it is bad, you still have time. You can get out."

At that moment, however, there was no way out. My mother had made it clear that I would be married, and there was nothing I could say or do to change her mind. Despite my objections, I conceded to her plan. Yet, I held her words close to my heart: "If it's bad, you can still get out."

I Won't Be a Child

May 16, 1991
11:00 p.m., Houston, Texas
(Summer in Houston before engagement)

I often wonder
What marriage will be like.
I often wonder
What changes will strike.

I will be no more
Of my parent's name,
But when I change
Won't I still be the same?

I won't be a child
Who spoke loud or had moods.
I won't be a child
Who demanded only certain foods.

I won't stomp my feet
To be pampered any longer.
I won't boss around and argue
Just to show I'm stronger.

I won't be a child
Who took long baths
And blew big bubbles.
I won't be a child
Who was mischievous
Always getting into troubles.

I won't be a child who sang out loud
And eagerly climbed trees.
I won't be a child
Who danced and played with the breeze.

Who will I be if not a child
When I change my name?
I'll begin another life
Which I know will never be the same.
I'll be a wife.

Agreeing to Go Forward

Weeks later, reluctantly, I met the boy-man my mother told me about. She asked him to come by our house by 5:00 p.m. and meet me so he could say whether he accepted me—not so I could say whether I accepted him. Although I should have been quite uneasy, considering we were in the same vacation house where all my trauma had happened, Mom was more anxious than I was. The house was clean, all the pillows on the couch were neatly arranged, and fresh incense filled the room with a sweet aroma just before his arrival. She had prepared *pohe*, a typical Maharashtrian dish made for guests, and was in the kitchen for a long time making sure everything for this meeting was just right.

I, on the other hand, was not interested in participating in her busyness. Seated quietly in a high-back chair, I glanced out the same window through which I'd seen the police officer lurking months earlier. Now, I waited for the next phase of my life to unfold, knowing I would soon open the same door I had slammed shut and stood numb before as my attacker stood on the opposite side. This time, I would let in another man, one who would possibly become my husband, my provider, my protector.

The entire scene was surreal as I went through the motions of preparing for something I should have been anticipating with joy, but instead was doing simply because I was told it was best for me. My brain was still foggy and stuck in the past, while my heart had completely shut down. Nervously, I stood up, humming a tune and swinging my arms to that rhythm to pass the time, uncertain of what to expect.

Glancing out the window, I saw him park his car and walk toward the front door. There was a calm yet confident presence about him. Good-looking and polished, tall and lanky, he carried himself with a careful disposition, and his attire reflected a sophisticated European influence. He came alone, which was unusual given that arranged marriages are mostly family affairs. Then again, the families had already done the preliminary discussions, and this meeting was intended for us to "get to know each other."

As I opened the door, he came inside. "Hello," was his simple greeting to me.

I replied with an American nod and smile, adding, "Hey," in a casual, unassuming tone.

I could sense my mother watching the curt exchange between us. She quickly appeared from the kitchen, asked us both to have a seat, and informed us she would be right back before she scurried off again.

There we were, he and I, just sitting there across from each other, awkwardly glancing around the room, afraid to look each other in the eyes. *What do I say? What is he supposed to say?* I was eighteen; he was twenty-two. We were kids. Neither of us had ever dated, but we were somehow expected to know how this meeting, this date, should work.

He was the eldest of his three siblings, the responsible one. *Well, there's one thing we have in common.* I knew well the sense of duty to family, the burden of expectations, and the weight of responsibility. He had a brother in engineering college and a sister my age in medical college. His father was a renowned pioneer of watershed management and irrigation and had dedicated his life to poverty-stricken, drought-prone villages in Maharashtra. The once thriving precision measuring instrument business he founded was in jeopardy. The young man in front of me was tasked with taking over the business and becoming the family breadwinner. His mother had also joined the company to hold the reins with her son. Work was his life; responsibility was his compass.

And then there was me, creative, bubbly, artistic, loud, adventurous, and always seeking a higher meaning to life. My effort at a casual conversation began with: "I love singing and teaching. I won numerous dance competitions in high school." He glanced at me, unimpressed, and I went on. "Then, I wanted to be an architect, but Dad insisted I follow an engineering or business path."

He appreciated that. He had attended the same business undergrad college I was attending at the time. Thankfully, that opened up the conversation. We talked about professors we both knew, since, he had just graduated with a bachelor's degree in commerce as I came into my first year in the same area of study. I was a vegetarian. He and his family preferred to be vegetarian but occasionally enjoyed a good green curried chicken. His mom was building a new home, which caught my interest, as architecture was a passion of mine.

Mom, of course, came in, after listening for the appropriate pause in our sentences, to place an array of food, tea, and water before us. Then, with a smile, she served us and quickly hurried back to the kitchen. There was no pretense of privacy. We were the key players in an arranged marriage, so practically all information was laid bare and everyone in the family was involved.

After an hour of small talk, he said, "Okay, well, I am going to leave now," speaking just loud enough for my mother to hear from her not-so-secret listening spot.

As he made his way toward the door, my mom walked through the kitchen over to where we stood. She held a bowl of sugar. "So what do you think?" she asked him with a big smile on her face. Traditionally, if the man takes a bit of sugar, it means he has accepted the woman's hand.

His family was more progressive than my traditional family was. Standing at the front door, I could tell he wasn't quite sure what to do. Out of respect and not to be rude when offered something, he took the sugar, and that was the official announcement that we were getting married. With no emotional connection to what would come next, I just went with it. *Oh, he accepted to marry me. I guess it's set then. What's next?*

A month later, Dad joined us in India. He met my potential betrothed and didn't say much. In fact, he never said anything about the attack at all, which made me angry. As it turned out, my mother hadn't told him what happened with the security guard. To this day, I believe he was unaware of what led to my mother insisting I get married. He likely just went along with her plan, assuming I also was eager to marry. Trapped in a culture and a family burdened with the tradition of silence, I took his hushed acceptance on the matter as yet another instance of his disapproval of me.

Although several family members were "on my side," and did express their objection to the marriage, including my dad, they did so for the wrong reasons. They compared my family's caste to his. He belonged to the Warrior caste, which was two levels down from ours. We are Brahmins, the top caste. Brahmins marry Brahmins. Warriors marry Warriors. It is frowned upon to mix castes, so although he was capable, he was not equivalent. Therefore, they believed he would not make a proper match. I despised discrimination, and out of anger at them all, I defiantly declared, "I will marry him."

Later that afternoon, as I passed the living room, where my dad sat, going through some work papers, he called out to me. "Hey, Rani, are you sure you want to marry him?" The question was so casual and unexpected, I almost didn't hear him.

Of course, I don't want to marry him or anyone else just yet. I looked back at him over my shoulder and said, "What do you mean, Baba?"

I was hoping for a real father-daughter conversation, maybe some guidance or empathy for what I'd recently experienced. Instead, he shrugged. "Well, number one, he's so skinny, he looks unhealthy and sick. And number two, he doesn't even belong to the same caste as us."

Number two was what got me. At that response, I gave my dad a snarky look, and snapped, "I'm marrying him." I whisked my head forward and walked up the stairs.

I had accepted my betrothed, not because I loved him and was ready to marry, but because he was being rejected by others. Rejection, after all, was familiar to me. By now, I had developed a keen distaste for unfairness, inequity, and favoritism. This was my way of taking a stand against rejection, but without realizing what I was setting myself up for. In that moment, however, reality hit me. My consent to marry, unnecessary as it was in this situation, was essentially the defining action that put plans into place for a marriage I didn't actually want for myself. My family didn't approve of it. My betrothed was simply doing what he thought was right. And I was defiantly walking into a future I didn't want. Despite all that, I felt it was too late to course correct. I was stuck. *What have I gotten myself into?*

The next day, I rode my motorbike to his workplace. When I walked into his office, bike helmet in hand, he was surprised and began fumbling with paperwork. "If we are going to be married," I said, "there are certain things we need to talk about." He agreed, and we met the next day at a local sandwich shop.

I drew on lessons I'd learned in business school for our negotiations. I had only two requirements for my soon-to-be husband: I had to finish my education and I had to keep singing. He agreed to both, and we consented to move forward with the marriage, albeit a year later, so I could finish my singing and complete as much school as I could.

Mom was overjoyed at my decision and started preparations for a grand wedding. Not surprisingly, I wasn't excited about my upcoming wedding, as most brides are. I didn't think about the guest list, seating arrangements, vows, or the perfect wedding bouquet. Although I was able to select what I wanted to wear, my mom chose the jewelry and all the events and activities associated with the ceremony. Because I'd had no say-so in choosing the groom, I had no interest in participating in the planning, other than what songs to sing or dance to.

Our official engagement, on July 4, 1991, was more of a public display, with rituals performed by a Hindu priest. In keeping with tradition, we exchanged rings, received presents, and had a big dinner with family. After that, I started spending more time with my soon-to-be in-laws.

They were wonderful. I loved them, and they loved to hear me sing, but I quickly grew tired of the monotony of it. Before the attack, my days had been filled with creative arts, meaningful debates, and teaching. Now that I was formally engaged, all that was gone. I was angry.

To add insult to injury, I learned the security guard who had assaulted me was still employed as a police officer. He had not been fired as promised by our family friends who initially recommended him to my mother. In fact, he accused me of coercing him, stating I was a modern, free-spirited, open-minded American girl who had even brought him flowers as a subtle invitation. His story was that I wanted his attention and when he gave in, I changed my mind. These were all lies, but as is so common, blaming the victim became the easy way out for the perpetrator.

About a month before my wedding day, I found myself in my room, burdened with the reality that was before me: a marriage I didn't want and the life that would follow. For hours, I sat in my room and cried. When Mom walked past, she saw me, came in, sat beside me, and asked, "What's wrong?"

I replied with my face down in my hands, "I don't think I can do this, Mom. This is just not for me, and I am not happy."

After a deep exhale, she shared words of Indian cultural wisdom. "Nothing will ever be perfect, Rani. Marriage is inevitable. You may never be ready because you won't know what ready feels like. Marriage is a gamble. But trust me, you will be fine."

That was new. I had never heard her say that. I lifted my head to see her face, but she looked away, as if her thoughts were somewhere else, maybe imagining how her life could have been different. "Marriage is tricky, even if you are in love," she said. "Sometimes it will work. Other times it will not." Although she and my father had chosen each other, somewhere along the way their relationship had fallen apart. They were an example that, in marriage, there are no guarantees.

She gazed directly into my eyes. "I want this to work out for you with all my heart. But if for any reason it doesn't, you are young. You will have time to get out."

She used those words again: "get out." Her desperate desire for more was as transparent as tracing paper. She wanted more for herself, but it seemed she was trapped. She had lost hope for her own way out of a broken marriage. She had made the decision to marry my father all those years ago and then realized it wasn't what she really wanted. My mom wanted more for me; I knew that. I wanted more for me as well, but here we were, so close to realizing what was expected of a young lady. So much was at stake now. A decision had been made, and I had agreed. So, instead of continuing to fight against it, I just acquiesced.

I gave Mom a hug and said, "I trust you. I know you want the best for me. I'll go ahead and give it my best."

At age nineteen, I was married, in December 1991, at my uncle's house with five hundred guests in attendance. When the time came, I walked down the aisle holding a long garland I would drape over my husband's head, signaling my acceptance of him. The garland sparked a warm remembrance of my childhood love for Krishna. But Krishna was long behind me. What laid before me was a sea of uncertainty, a future I was afraid to know but was destined to experience.

As I approached the altar, gasps and exhales of joy spread through the air. Our family and friends admired my sari, my hair, and my slow, graceful procession toward the altar. They assumed I was giddy with anticipation of the new role I would step into, but I wasn't. I should have been forward focused, but my mind was elsewhere. Less than a foot from the altar, I paused and turned to look behind me, hoping someone would relieve me of the need to continue with this charade. Even my *aaji* had no say in the matter. She was present, and we'd briefly held hands to take pictures prior to the ceremony. Three generations of women—she, my mom, and I—stood shoulder-to-shoulder, beautiful and proud, yet each with our own uncertainties about the future. I looked up to my aaji.

She'd whispered, as she gently released my hand, "*Rana Pratap, Je kahi karshil, changalch karshil.*" Whatever I did, she assured me, she knew I would do my best. At that moment, all I could do was nod and give her a half smile. As heartfelt as her intention might have been, her words did little to ease the anxiety I felt before taking the long stroll down the aisle.

Steps from the altar, I scanned the room for somebody to pull me back and say, "You don't have to do this. Come back." I wanted one person to say, "Stop. I got you. Let's just go home." But no one came forward. No one was going to save me. I wanted to run, but where would I go? I was already in my uncle's house, and all our family and friends were watching. I couldn't disappoint them all and bring shame to the family. I had to follow through.

Most brides don't look behind them and grieve what they are leaving, but I did. I loved my family and felt I was being separated from them. Saying goodbye to something so good and familiar was difficult. I had convinced myself that standing up for equality was more important than my own happiness.

Taking one final deep breath and exhaling a gentle "Om" to hide the pain of bidding a final farewell to all my plans, aspirations, and dreams, I turned to face my future and fixed my eyes forward. When my foot hit the ground to take the next step, tears of sadness and acceptance filled my eyes. I felt helpless and disappointed. Every step I took brought me closer to the realization that nobody was going to help me, and nobody understood who I was.

Throughout my many years of being alone—as an only child, as the eldest sibling understood by no one in my family, and finally as a young woman, growing secure within myself and finding the pathway to my self-defined future—nothing came close to this feeling of absolute inner isolation. In that moment, my happiness was nowhere to be found. I wanted to run, escape, and make my own path. Instead, I tearfully walked in surrender, slowly losing my sense of me.

Standing there before our guests, with the curtain drawn between me and my husband-to be, I listened to the priest chant. Finally, everyone threw their rice blessings upon us, an indication of their hope for abundance and a fruitful future. The curtain dropped, and everyone awaited my next act with anticipation. The bride is supposed to put the garland over the man, but I couldn't. I stood frozen, unable to move my arms in the simple gesture to welcome my new husband into my life.

After a few seconds, a lady standing behind me tapped me on the shoulder. "Okay, Rani, you can go ahead now," she said. Still, I didn't move. I was crying, sobbing uncontrollably. Surely, the guests believed I was overcome with the sweet emotion of joy, but that was not the truth. My mother's words rang in my mind: "You're young. You can still get out." I needed to run away now, but my body rebelled and remained motionless.

Another tap on the other shoulder brought me back to the present. "It's okay, Rani," the voice urged. Still, I didn't move. Someone finally lifted my elbow and helped me put the garland over his head. I never once looked at him. I was stuck in the moment, my eyes glued shut, tears streaming down my face, body unmoving for a moment. There was no turning back.

Finally, the ceremony was complete and all in attendance were joyous—all except me. For the next two hours, I carried on with the remainder of the rituals and traditions; however, I had emotionally checked out. Following the festivities, I packed my bags and moved into my husband's room in the home he shared with all the members of his family. There I was, one short year after my mother arrived in India, a married woman. I had transitioned to the land of adulthood, where I would be identified and judged by my role as a wife.

Out of nowhere, the winds of my future had changed. The expression of my spirit went from free, confident, and happy to responsible, surrendering, and quiet. From then on, everyone around me made choices about how I should be and what I should do. In that season of my life, my understanding was that the only way forward was to suppress my power to choose; however, my core nature would continue to find reasons to smile and be creative within the boundaries set by those in my life. In an instant, my phase of innocent youth had closed, and the uncertainty of adulthood had begun.

Dearest Daughters,

Oh, my precious, if I could just wipe your tears. So much pushing, pulling, and somehow trying to make it through as best as you know. You've seen some cool triumphs, but then the defeats overtook the things you held close. I know it's not easy and your heart hurts. Decisions were made for you, and still people made you believe you chose that way. I guess in a way you did, huh. You surrendered, you let go, you let life take you in whichever direction it wanted for you. So much uncertainty and noise, yet your spirit is the most quiet and motionless.

It's the hardest to move from youth to adulthood. You feel like you have to lose so much of what you knew. You are not losing your identity. Instead, you are being molded for a greater purpose that will reveal itself later. It sure feels unfair, but you know well, we cannot judge no matter how much we want to. You tapped into happy and freedom once when you were my little young one, and then somehow, suddenly got stuck.

My dearest, Love is still around, stable, and strong. It's also shifting with you, adapting with you. Really it is. Love will show up in different ways to protect you and give you courage to build you for your every need. Love now widens its net to catch all that is required as you start your journey into the big picture of this world.

The quiet within is where Love lives. That Love will lead you to adapt through all the questions you won't find immediate answers to or the times when you won't know in which direction to go. But the good news is, all the goodness and love that you have been still exists in you. You are still you, empathetic and truthful. Listen to yourself as you do to others. Hear what is being said, and not said. You are learning how to pause, which will become your power when the time comes to make your choices and stand by them. When life sends these pauses, it is a sign of a shift.

Seasons change and before they do, there will be a lull, a space where all elements adapt to the new. Within that space there is a quiet, where nothing moves. This is where you can breathe, my dear. Breathe. Listen. Get ready to watch Love unfold and support your decisions. Much is on its way.

Love always,
Rani

Chapter Four:

WHEN I BECAME A MOTHER
TWENTY-ONE TO TWENTY-EIGHT YEARS OLD

Cause and effect, means and ends,
seed and fruit cannot be severed; the fruit is in the seed.
~ Ralph Waldo Emerson

For seven years, I was a wife in name and practice. I settled into my duties in an automatic, involuntary way. I entered my marriage focused on what I didn't want to change about my life, rather than on what was rapidly transforming in front of me. I wasn't excited about marriage or about my new husband, but I always maintained a happy disposition, always smiling and available to serve whatever need the household had.

As tradition dictated, I was expected to be a certain way and, although I could not express my inner youth and curiosities, I found ways to stay active, creative, and joyful. Eventually, almost by hypnotic suggestion, I became sanguine, convinced that this was the path I had to take, regardless of my own still cloudy desires.

My new husband and I lived in a joint family home. A foreign concept for most Westerners but quite common in India, in this living arrangement, parents, grandparents, children, aunts, and uncles share a family home. With many people in one home, it was a challenge to find personal and private time. I had to let go of my rigorous vocal training schedule. I became a master multi-tasker and found ways to manage numerous activities and responsibilities in order to carve time out to sing.

My husband's family was wealthy, influential, and highly visible in the city's high society. For them, higher education was a mark of sophistication and achievement, so neither my husband nor my in-laws had any issue with my pursuit of an undergraduate degree. Hindustani Indian classical vocal, to which I was devoted, is a respected and respectable art form in India and, therefore, was a perfectly suitable passion for the wife of a well-positioned man. With these fragments of satisfaction and creative outlet, I went about as if my life could continue as it had been, as if my marriage, unwelcome as it was initially, need not change everything about my existence. I couldn't have been more wrong.

Becoming a Lioness to a Cub

I once saw a nature documentary that followed a pride of lions and a particular lioness and her two small cubs. The camera lingered on the lioness as she relaxed among the tall, amber-colored grass, while her cubs wrestled and frisked nearby. She led them to watering holes and watched them clumsily swim. She brought her kills to them and watched silently as they ate. Constantly observant, yet unobtrusive, the lioness ensured her cubs developed all the skills they needed to survive on the African savanna. When they stumbled, she remained patient and still, waiting for them to get up and try again. She allowed them to take risks and to fail, but the moment a genuine threat appeared on the horizon, everything changed in the lioness.

Suddenly, a male lion appeared nearby—rangy, golden, and up to no good—stalking the cubs as they tumbled and teased one another, unaware of the danger. The ever-watchful lioness raised her head in a protective gaze. In one swift and incredible leap, she put herself between the interloper and her cubs, springing into action, coiled and tense. As the lioness stared down the threatening lion, she communicated what he already knew; she would fight to the death to protect her offspring. Within a few minutes, the male lion turned and sauntered away, his tail flicking the top of the tall grass, as the lioness padded gently back to her position, content to watch her cubs from a distance once more.

The instinct of motherhood is the same for woman and beast. We lie in wait, ready to pounce on anyone and anything that threatens to harm our young. Then, as quickly as we tense up, we shift and relax when the danger is gone, lovingly focusing on our offspring. The lioness will always protect her cub. Without a doubt, I was a lioness.

I was pregnant before our first anniversary. I was twenty years old, in my third and final year of college, and like so much of what happened with my body, my pregnancy was somewhat mysterious to me. I knew as much about reproduction as I had known about menstruation or sexuality before I was confronted with those changes, which is to say, virtually nothing. I didn't want to be a mother, at least not at that time in my life. I was still reeling from the abrupt and violent end of my ladyhood. Adding a baby to this turmoil felt impossible.

During my first appointment with the family doctor, I was ambivalent. When I asked about terminating the pregnancy, the doctor, a woman, gravely told me that if I had an abortion, I would never be able to have children again. Disrupting my first pregnancy, she explained, would destroy my ability to conceive in the future. I had no way of knowing what the doctor told me was a lie intended to limit my options for what to do with my own body. As a result of my inexperience, I believed her and went about preparing for a new life to enter my world.

Once again, I found myself pushed and pulled along by the powerful currents of a life increasingly beyond my control. Although abortion is very common in India, my husband insisted we have the child. Like my father, he saw his firstborn as a vital part of his legacy. Quite likely, he believed, as my mother had with regard to my father, that a baby would cement us together, creating a living, breathing connection between two people struggling to bond. For me, the choice wasn't between having a child and not having a child, but between having this child at this moment and never being a mother at all. I chose to continue the pregnancy and begin my journey into motherhood, however rocky and unpredictable it might turn out to be.

I didn't feel ready to be a mother, but as my body began to change, I warmed to my new physical reality. I discovered there was something genuinely beautiful about being pregnant. It didn't have anything to do with people giving up seats on public transportation or smiling more in public, the social softening that sometimes comes with being visibly pregnant. Instead, it was something that happened purely inside me.

My acceptance of motherhood began the first time the baby quickened, and I felt her fluttering kicks. Suddenly, this tiny spark within became real for me—a small person growing and developing inside my body. As I accepted that a new life was forming inside me, I talked to her often. I felt from the very beginning that she was a she, a daughter, *my* daughter. I called her, *Mana*, my mind, and had endless conversations with her about the world and who she might become. Thankfully, my husband did not feel the same way my father had about daughters being inferior to sons.

My emotional experience of becoming a mother can't be untangled from the physical experience. There is a tremendous power in carrying a child in your womb, of being so intimately connected to another being, while also remaining a distinct entity. Every physical decision I made included a silent, but certainly not motionless, party. I felt a tremendous sense of responsibility for her with everything I did. As her armor, I enfolded and surrounded her, becoming the filter through which she experienced a world she had never seen. Unsurprisingly, my first sense of what it meant to be a mother was about protection.

I was more than just a shield; I was also a resource. My body provided her with all the nourishment she needed to build herself from the smallest of cells. I was food, water, and oxygen to her. More than that, though, I was her first ambassador of love in the world, the first person to communicate with her, the first person to show her affection, to sing to her, to talk to her, to comfort her. My job was to show her what it meant to be loved. That mission was humbling and exciting. I was determined my daughter would understand not only love, but also joy and freedom, three things I'd struggled for in my own childhood.

As the eldest sister, I'd assumed the role I would play as a mother would essentially be the same as my role with my siblings. Sure, I would be able to make more of the rules and probably be less irritated when bringing my own child along on outings, but the basic feeling would be the same, I thought. I quickly realized the feeling of motherhood is an order of magnitude stronger than what I felt as a sister. The sense of responsibility was intense. The love was so powerful it sometimes felt all-consuming.

As I taught myself how to mother, I thought often about the lioness and her cubs. The lioness became a role model for me. I wanted to give my child what she gave hers, space to grow within an aura of protection. To do that, I had to learn how to stand back and wait—how to distinguish momentary challenges my daughter should solve herself from true dangers that required my intervention.

My husband was quite traditional in his approach to fatherhood. Children and pregnancy were the province of women. His job was to work and provide. As soon as I decided not to get an abortion, my husband lost most of his interest in my pregnancy and in me. Like the lioness, I experienced motherhood as a mostly solitary condition. I had a sense of insularity, as though my daughter and I were a unit unto ourselves. We were our own pride.

I completed my undergraduate degree during my pregnancy, even sitting for final exams in my sixth month. I was so big by that point that I couldn't fit into the benches in the examination hall and had to get a waiver to write my exam in a teacher's lounge where there was a single chair and a separate desk. Despite the struggles I faced in the last six months of the program, I passed with honors.

Like my mother, I wanted to have my baby in a place that felt like home, which for me, was Houston. My husband was pleased with this idea because it meant our daughter would have American citizenship. I was more concerned about having my mother with me and about the wider array of birthing options available at an American hospital. Like my mother, I headed back to my home country alone to give birth.

Money didn't keep my husband from joining me; his work did. While there were early hints of trouble in our marriage, this was the first major sign of a problem that would eventually cause deep fractures. He made it clear that his business was his top priority, even over the birth of our first child. That pattern would hold for the duration of our marriage.

To his credit, my husband did make an attempt to come to Houston. But as he explained, he was extremely busy, so if I could give him an exact date when the baby would arrive, it would be easier for him to plan a flight. Of course, I couldn't tell him exactly when our daughter would be born. I had not planned a C-section or inducement, so I gave him the due date the doctors had given me and cautioned him that it was not exact. He promised he would plan accordingly.

The week I was due, my husband called to let me know he couldn't come. "Do you think you can hold on?" he asked, as if childbirth was as simple a thing to reschedule as an oil change or a virtual meeting.

I didn't know much about giving birth, but I did know it wasn't a matter of holding on and holding in. Rather than berate him for his ill-informed planning, I slowly said, "I guess?" because there seemed to be nothing else I could do or say. In retrospect, this seemed an appropriate circumstance for my becoming a mother because the experience was something of an analogy for motherhood as a whole.

When I went into labor, a few days later, my husband was still in India. My labor lasted two days and the contractions seemed to take forever to get close enough that I could head to the hospital. I languished at home for most of the first day, my doting mother at my side, breathing with me through the worst physical pain I'd ever felt. The only thing that helped soothe both the physical pain and the emotional anxiety I experienced were affirmations and music. The soft tones of the Indian bamboo flute flowed like a stream and steadied my breath. It offered me peace, calmness, and a gentle mindset to look forward without worry or question, with hope and love.

When I headed in for delivery and finally received an epidural, my baby abruptly stopped moving. She wasn't progressing down the birth canal, and my labor slowed. Doctors and nurses flurried around me, discussing which intervention was appropriate. Eventually, they decided to reach in with forceps and pull my reluctant daughter into the world. As she descended, she suddenly gave an almighty kick—so hard it cracked my tailbone. With that final thrust, Bhakti was born.

Two days later, my husband arrived with apologies and excuses. By that time, I didn't even have it in me to be upset. I had known when she was still in the womb that I would need to protect myself, to guard my heart from disappointment. I used this self-erected firewall frequently, which allowed me to push away any animosity I felt toward my husband and focus all my love and attention on my daughter. She and I were a team, and we would have to work together to get through whatever came next. Bhakti forged me into something new, yet another version of myself I would never have discovered alone. Bhakti means "devotion," and the name was apt. From the moment I saw her, I was devoted to her.

Despite my strong bond with my daughter, motherhood was difficult. One of the toughest lessons I had to learn was to care for someone else when I was hurting in so many ways. I couldn't sit for the first three months of her life while my tailbone healed. I wasn't able to breastfeed her. However, like the lioness, I had an almost primal sense of responsibility toward my child. *You are first. You are always first.*

After Bhakti was born, I chose to pause my entry into the workforce and care for her full time. Even then, managing time became more of a challenge. A baby's needs are unpredictable. Once her world was taken care of, I had a tiny window to practice and compose music. Singing with her on my hip or as she lay in her crib nearby didn't allow me the intensity I needed to practice. Time slid by, and I began to feel my years of hard work and persistence to excel in the craft I loved had summed up to nothing. Singing was my first love and the one thing I negotiated to keep throughout my marriage as mine. I adored my baby girl, but a part of me—the little girl who sang inside me and who gave me a sense of who I was in this world—was put aside. I felt lost.

Another love waited on the sidelines, however. During the many years when singing was at the forefront, I hadn't utilized my extensive dance background. I was proficient in ballet and the Indian classical dance styles of Bharatnatyam and Kathak, and I loved gymnastics and yoga. This part of me was about to be set free.

Bhakti

June 22, 2001
8:00 p.m., Pune, India
(Bhakti growing up)

Wrapped in a bow
Her hair gracefully flows.
Her mind has care,
Balanced—everywhere.

Curiosity, creativity,
Depth, love, and play
Innocence reigns
Wondrous of mine
Touching the sun, moon,
Galaxies of stars every day.

The Art of Expression

Bhakti was a happy child, always excited to go places. Her curly black hair bounced with her smile. The front basket of my bicycle was her favorite place to sit while we enjoyed the breeze brushing against our cheeks and the tailwind helping us go faster. She was a breath of fresh air, carefree and silly. And I could be the same with her. I imagined our relationship was much like my relationship with my mother when I was young, when we played together and could be ourselves, unburdened by responsibility or roles or expectations for a little while.

To provide Bhakti with quality playtime during which she could make friends, I organized and taught summer camps. When she turned four and we began considering preschool, I was torn. On the one hand, I wanted her to be independent, to learn and grow and interact with other children. And on the other hand, like the lioness in the grass, I felt a deep need to keep an eye on Bhakti, watchful and ready in case of danger.

After I dropped her off at the all-girls school on her first day, I took a moment to glance back and watch her mix and mingle. There she was, giggling, skipping to class, carefree and innocent. On either side of the front entry gate stood security guards. At an all-girls school, guards were everywhere. Guards. I paused in my tracks. My stomach and chest tightened, and my breath shifted deeper. I didn't trust security guards and the farther she went into the schoolyard, the faster my heart raced. *Will she be protected? Will her kind voice be overpowered by others or our cultural traditions?* I had to find a way to protect my cub. I needed to be close to her.

Silently, I followed Bhakti into the school, deciding to approach the principal with my sudden idea.

"Hello. I'm Bhakti's mother. Today is her first day," I explained, hoping not to sound desperate. "I wonder if there is any way I can help here at the school."

"Well," she said, sizing me up, "Do you have any talents?"

I told her about my classical singing and mentioned I also did some dancing.

"Could you teach dance?" she asked.

"Sure," I said, sharing how I was classically trained in several dance forms and could team popular Bollywood and Indian folk dances if that was desired. I knew I could pull something together.

"The older girls have a concert coming up in four months," the principal said. "We wouldn't be able to pay you."

Payment was of no concern to me. I simply wanted to be near my daughter every day. The icing on the cake would be that I could indulge my love of movement and self-expression. The opportunity seemed ideal, so I became a dance teacher.

The day I was to meet my first group of girls at the school, I was excited, expecting the sounds of girlish laughter and rustling feet to enter the room. Instead, my class of nearly forty seventh-graders walked in, quiet and expressionless, their faces stiff, their shoulders hunched over. A teacher escorted them and introduced me. The girls responded in a rehearsed sing-song unison, "Good morning, teacher."

They were obedient, knew what to say and how to say it. But their energies were suppressed, pushed down through their slouchy posture. It seemed they were scared to speak. Seeing them this way saddened me, probably because it reminded me of myself when I was told what to do and say and had no voice of my own. They reminded me of the woman I'd helped in India who was afraid to speak to her husband. She'd needed my fourteen-year-old hand to help her find her voice.

Growing up as an elder sister with empathy for my siblings and now as a mother with the innate need to nurture, I wanted to extend my hand again, this time to other fourteen-year-olds, to help them find their voice. I welcomed the challenge and tried to get some movement going. In an excited voice, I exclaimed, "Well, good morning, girls! It's so nice to see you. How about we dance a few steps?" Without much noise, they followed me like puppets. No expression, no life, no feeling.

Trying a different approach, I asked, "Do you have any steps to show me?"

Strangely, a hush filled the room. The silence was deafening, unusual, considering what I know to be true of girls: we love to talk. Finally, one girl chirped, "We will follow you."

I felt defeated. That wasn't at all the reply I hoped for. Yet, with each of the three classes that day, I was met with the same stoic, robotic response from the young girls. When each class ended, the girls left without a giggle or a smile, a sad, troubling reality I was determined to rectify.

As I reflected on the first day of classes, I marveled at how God always seemed to put me in front of these large groups of children. It was a challenge, but it was one I knew I could meet. My task was multilayered. On the surface, I needed to teach the students to memorize and perform a choreographed dance. In a deeper sense, although I wanted them to enjoy the class, I needed to inspire them to *want* to learn, not just about a specific dance, but about movement in general. Ultimately, I hoped they would become confident girls who felt a sense of accomplishment and understood they were valuable, that their voices and opinions mattered.

This new job provided an opportunity to share something I loved with young people, something that would inspire and transform their lives. I hadn't been in a situation like this since I'd formed my impromptu school at the vacation house, and I was surprised by how good it felt. With that, I enacted a new approach to teaching. I would start by learning about the students, and so I began my classes not with instructions, but with questions.

The next day, I invited them to sit down so we could talk before dancing. My first question: "How are you today?"

I received the same sing-song response again. "Good morning, teacher. We are fine."

This had to change. I asked each girl individually about the music we used and the individual steps in the dance. "What did you think when you did this dance? Which step was your favorite? What movements made you happy?"

At first, they struggled to express how they felt. Soon, there were some nods and a few answers. Women and girls in Indian society, as in most societies, are often discouraged from speaking up. Retribution for doing so takes many forms, including being labeled impudent or strident or even being physically attacked. It can be dangerous for girls to use their voices. Yet, each time a student offered her shy reply to my questions, I smiled and gave her a high five, which encouraged them all to express how they felt.

Tenth grade is the conclusion of high school in India. Most of these children were preparing to face adulthood, despite being only fourteen or fifteen. There wasn't much space in their lives for silliness or fun; however, I was in a position to provide that for them. Dance is often seen as a safe, appropriate form of female expression. As a form of communication, dance is every bit as complex and intricate as any spoken language. Every movement, every choice is infused with meaning and intention. To dance is to speak, to connect, to give, and to receive.

For most of the girls, my classroom was the only place they could express their true feelings, where someone actually listened to them. Many times I heard girls say things like, "I'm going to be an engineer, but I don't really want to. I love to sew." Or "I wish I could be an architect, but my parents say I have to be a doctor because that's where the money is." These were not abstract concerns. They were real-life choices these girls would soon have to make.

They were picking their colleges and majors in obedience to the wishes of their families, not according to the desires of their heart. That they were pushed at a very young age to take on extremely grown-up responsibilities, while not being allowed to make their own decisions seemed unfair to me. How often I'd found my own life choices neatly cut and served to me as the trajectory of my life unfolded.

Once again, facing the reality of how the world views girls and women, I was even more determined to provide a safe space for these girls before their lives became fully dictated by others. In my class, at least for an hour each day, they could experience the freedom to explore, to play, and to fully be themselves. As the week progressed, the start of each class got louder and gigglier. After the bouts of laughter, we began choreography. A few weeks later, the giggles turned into conversation.

The girls had something to say. They had a voice and a choice. Dance was about them, and I was dancing alongside them. Their new behavior reminded me of a quote by Albert Camus that I learned about as a child from Winnie the Pooh, my favorite Zen wisdom character. "Don't walk behind me for I may not lead. Don't walk in front of me for I may not follow. Just walk beside me and be my friend." Then, I added, so we can journey ahead together.

And that's what we did. We moved forward together. When I helped them, I was also helping myself, and because of them, I was finding myself. I developed leadership games where they listened to and respected one another. As we rehearsed the dance routines, I encouraged them to personalize the experience, whenever possible, maintaining the timing and rhythm of the group yet adding their own flair. If a girl wanted to bring in her own music or to try out her own choreography, I encouraged her to do just that. I happily rewarded them for every effort they made to reveal their individuality. In a short time, my classroom became a place where the girls could meet on equal ground, where they could have a say, and where they could express their true selves.

Finally, the day of the grand annual performance arrived. All the girls danced with beauty and pride, each showcasing the hours of time and intention she had poured into the movements. At the end of the show, the parents thanked me. Some said they hadn't seen their daughter so happy in a long time. They said I made a positive difference, and I was humbled. I merely wanted to be around my own daughter and was blown away with the many daughters I had gained. More girls were being empowered to stand together. More girls felt safe using their voice. I had helped to protect their choice. An eternal spark had been lit within me and no matter where, I would continue teaching. I had found my purpose.

Wherever I taught, my students could be fierce, joyful, or luminous; they could speak their hearts through the movement of their bodies. They didn't simply speak to a passive audience either; we answered one another. Dance formed a community, established bonds, opened the door to leadership and friendship outside the bubble in which many girls and women, including myself, had spent their life.

An incredible power comes from using the human body in artistic ways. My struggle with accepting my appearance didn't go away when I got married. Dance allowed me to see my face and body not as unsatisfactory or undesirable, but as tools and mediums of inspiration. *I may not be pretty, but my dancing is pretty. People love the way my body moves with the music and get joy from watching me dance.* Knowing I had the skill, the influence, and the gift to impact others in such a way, was powerful to me. Not only could I create through dance, but I could also create life through my body. After all, my body had brought forth a beautiful daughter whom I cherished dearly. *My body can do and give so much, so it can't be bad.*

This was the transformation I needed to move forward in my life. I wanted to give that transformative feeling to others so they could embrace the beauty of their own forms and use that beauty to express themselves. Not every young woman would be able to follow her dreams or pursue the career she wanted, but I was certain

I could at least give them a safe space to consider what they truly wanted from life.

When Bhakti was four, I established a dance company called ISHA, Indian Search for Harmony through Art, which I later changed to Integral Search for Harmony through Art. As the name implies, I wanted to help young women integrate self-expression into their lives, to provide a safe platform where they could speak freely, express their dreams, and find their unique selves, translating thought into movement through the art of dance. We began with modern dance ballets because that had always been my forte, a more classical, elegant style.

Over time, we evolved to include other dance forms. The school provided base choreography, but the concept, design, and execution were student facilitated. Within eighteen months, our group of forty girls, ages nine to fourteen, performed the first-of-its-kind Broadway-style contemporary Indian dance program.

The colorful and lively production took place at a renowned auditorium in the center of the city with a full house of three thousand people in attendance and a backstage crew of about twenty. From there, the performances took off, and we performed Broadway shows nearly every month for a year. Then, we started competing in local, state, and countrywide competitions. Each year saw a gradual increase in the quality and size of performances. Never had I dreamed of this kind of exponential growth, but I embraced it and enjoyed every moment. My youthful spirit thrived with the young performers. The energy we shared was natural, exciting and freeing; it felt like home.

The programs I developed expanded beyond the original focus on young girls. They spread across Pune, parts of Mumbai, and outside India. ISHA's methodology of using dance and natural body movements as a medium of expression and leadership impacted teens, college students, adults, corporate teams, and even the blind and deaf. The more I helped to empower, the more empowered I became. My eyes were set on building a stand-alone facility for complete wellness.

By this time in my life, I had experienced a spiritual evolution. I had developed my own personal style of dance, which I called Elemental Movement, rooted in my understanding of the five elements—air, water, earth, fire, and space—and how they interacted. I had long since moved on from my veneration of Krishna, though he would always hold a special place in my heart. By now, God had become a more abstract creature, holding a place somewhere "out there," yet without a name or any defining characteristics. Still, I felt his power and work in the world and within me. When singing and performing on stage, I always felt a deep and moving connection with God, a synching of spirit and body that put me at peace. Whether I danced, taught, or spoke in front of hundreds, I was in my pure element, a sacred zone of flow.

Having a Second Child

The more invested I became in dance, the more deeply I explored the spiritual elements of movement. I wanted to use my art to explore my beliefs in a more personal way, to link dance and spirituality, and I wanted to offer that to my students as well.

My school was a platform to reach girls of all ages and economic situations, from various family backgrounds and with different interests, body types, and abilities. I wanted to sweep them up, protect them, and provide for them the way I had done for my own biological daughter. My identity as a mother encompassed all the daughters who came to me. As my company grew, I even started to attract the attention of older women, housewives who hadn't danced since they were children, if at all. I discovered then that even grown-ups can occasionally use some mothering and encouragement.

As the business grew and I took on more roles, I realized my own Bhakti was becoming increasingly isolated. She had inherited many of my quirks. While she enjoyed the same vivid imagination and rich inner life as I'd had at her age, she also had the same struggles with relinquishing control to others. She was a perfect example of the apple not falling far from the tree. When she wasn't at school, she tended to stay in her room and play quietly with her toys, preferring her own games over the company of others. Although I understood it was possible to be happy and alone, that was never something I wanted for my daughter. In my efforts to introduce more engagement with other children, I even started summer camps so Bhakti would have friends her age.

Bhakti was with me the majority of the time. During the rare times we were apart, she was often with my mom, an ideal place of love and family. My youngest sister, Sayali, was only four years older than Bhakti, so they made a great team. However, over time, learning to create room for someone else was a struggle for my daughter. Even apologizing was a hard task for her. I understood that, to some degree, these characteristics were common to an only child, but I soon became concerned.

My husband and I had never been in love, and our union wasn't exactly happy. We were merely content. By the time Bhakti was six, we were no longer at our best. As much as my dance company was about teaching and leading, it also became my escape. I had begun to build my life around the times when I could get out of the house for an assignment, practice, or performance. I would complete the tasks expected of me at home, as though checking them off a list, and then, as soon as I could, I would flee to be with my girls. I was almost never happy at home. When I found some joy in the world, I grabbed for it with both hands, just as I had always done.

Realizing the turn my life had taken, I started to think deeply about my marriage and whether it was sustainable. When I saw my daughter—already so much like me—disappearing into the same insular, private world I had created as a child, I feared she would end up like me, alone, even amongst family. Spending time alone was not a problem, but it was not easy, and I didn't want my child to go through the pain of figuring life out on her own. The only solution I could come up with was that she needed a sibling.

My husband and I had not taken advantage of our other opportunities to have a second child. It was not customary for married couples to use contraception, and I only had a basic understanding of reproduction and how to prevent pregnancy. As a result, I did have other pregnancies. With each one, I grew angrier that the doctor had lied to me years earlier about abortions to exert control over me, my body, and my decisions about my own life.

A couple years after Bhakti was born, I became pregnant again. Knowing I was not ready for another child, and that I was already struggling to keep my head afloat in my current mind frame, I informed my husband of my pregnancy and that I planned to have an abortion. He didn't try to dissuade me, so I packed myself into a rickshaw, went to the doctor alone, got an abortion, and went home. Later that night, I put on one of my nicest saris and prepared for a dinner gathering hosted in our home for some important people in the city. My husband and I never spoke of the abortion. I didn't complete the pregnancy because I was never fully settled into my marriage.

Having one child seemed to change everything about terminating additional pregnancies. Whether one child simply indicated to the world our ability to procreate or it solidified an heir to our legacy, I'm unsure. But with the subsequent pregnancies, my husband no longer cared one way or the other whether the child was born. He said the choice was up to me. Similarly, my doctor never again mentioned any harmful effects from the procedure or any potential loss of fertility. It was as though once I had Bhakti and had proven my marriage was "successful" (or at least fruitful), it no longer mattered to anyone what I did with my body. I had fulfilled my purpose as a wife and checked one more task off the list.

Bhakti was intended to cement and legitimize our union, but she deserved a life of happiness, one she didn't have to endure as an only child. I wondered if a second child would be too much for me, especially considering I was also expected to manage all the domestic and social aspects of our life. I wasn't sure I wanted to divide my focus while Bhakti was still young, yet I began to feel I was denying her some necessary part of the human experience by not having another child.

I knew as well as anyone that sibling relationships could be complicated, but I also knew they created a bond unlike anything else. A sibling often provides the intimacy of family without the sometimes-extreme power differential of the parent-child relationship. Looking back at my own childhood, I vividly remember the feeling of being on a team, of having other people in the world who could understand where I had come from because they had come from the same place.

In 2000, when I was twenty-eight years old, I had my second daughter. The funny thing about pregnancies—and about children—is that each one is unique. I thought I knew what to expect when I had my second child, but it was almost completely different from the first time. Even the birth experience was the complete opposite of my ordeal with Bhakti. My second daughter came dashing into the world, just one hour after my labor began. I could barely believe it was over so soon.

When I had Bhakti, I was little more than a young lady myself. My parents sent my youngest sister, Sayali, when she was three years old, to stay with me in the early days of my marriage, since my mother was exhausted and needed a break. In many ways, it still felt like I was playing the big sister to two rambunctious girls a few years apart, rather than being a mom to one. I felt as though Bhakti and I had grown up together. When her sister came along, my mothering self was more mature, more experienced. I felt more comfortable in my role. Again, I was the lioness, guiding her little ones through their perilous youth.

We named my second daughter Sharayu, which means "flowing like the breeze." I thought a lot about the names I gave my children. I wanted each to reflect what I wanted for them. When I chose the name Sharayu, I was thinking about kites, the different types and designs and fabrics. The possibilities are endless. Each one is a work of art, beautiful, delicate, and colorful. They are powerful creations built by hand and then taken out into the world where they're just let go. Of course, you watch the wind carefully, you give them a running start, and you remain at the end of a tether to give them guidance or support.

The purpose of making a kite is to watch it fly away from you, to help it soar and be free. That was what I wanted for my Sharayu and Bhakti. I wanted them to fly high and free. I wanted them to do what they were made to do, to dance and flicker and gleam in the sun, but most importantly, to know balance—not just how high to fly but when to rest, how to recharge and set off again. Whichever phase of flight they were in, I would be available, at the end of a tether as long or as short as they wanted it to be, a safe and welcoming place for when they returned to the earth.

Sharayu

October 7, 2000

11:30 p.m., Houston, Texas

(Nine months pregnant with Sharayu)

While I lie here
Soul in soul
I wonder about life,
Fold in fold.

One cannot I see
One comes from me
Past living in the sea
What now is to be?

Strength vibrates
Justice initiates
Peace perseveres
Balance emancipates.

Special is to be
This one of one,
To shine upon
Like the only sun.

Took its time
Chosen to its cater
Am I the home
Of this history maker?

May I do the best
To listen, raise, and lead
For I believe
This is a precious seed.

Dearest Daughters,

I see you are set to fly! Oh, what joy it is to watch you become independent and face your ambitions, love, and even fears with a can-do attitude. And oh, those relationships. Each one, including the more special intimate ones, is where you will find love receiving. You are feeling wanted and loved, and you are beginning to see your true self through some else's eyes. It is a beautiful, precious feeling. But remember, the words and gestures from other people are there to cherish yes, but also to allow you to see who you are. You see, people are reflecting who you are. They are essentially you. As Love receives, it accepts, and loves every part of you.

The butterflies in your belly, the excitement in your tone as you speak, and the slight impatience to get things done so you can be with your loved ones are all signs that Love is receiving its essence and you are filling up. Can you feel its power? It empowers you to share, inspire, motivate, and even help heal others.

Not all relationships will be forever, but each will have meaning and will be true at that moment for both of you. Honestly, there is no fault or looking back into how something could be better or not. When Love receives, it does so without any agenda. It is just energy, transforming from one to the next. So, for any reason, if the energy in a relationship lessens or enhances, Love will make its way accordingly. Through it all, do remember, you are constant, you are true as are all people around. Each is living their own truth.

Each relationship will have its own intensity and depth. Accordingly, you will know why and how Love leads you to react or not. In other words, Love will enable you to decide how close or distant to be with a person, all in due respect and dignity.

Lessons become complex and tougher. You are climbing upwards, where simple may not always be available. But let Love make the jour-

ney easier for you. You are now beginning to plant seeds for your future. It's the beginning of your legacy. What you choose, how you choose, and why will determine how that choice affects someone else's life. And when your actions impact someone else, you have started building your foundations to legacy, even if you don't understand how your action is changing someone else. Come home whenever you need to rest and reflect. My love is always here for you.

Love always,
Rani

Chapter Five:

WHEN I BECAME A WIFE
TWENTY-EIGHT TO THIRTY-FIVE YEARS OLD

Thirty spokes share the hub of a wheel;
yet it is its center that drives the chariot.
~ Tao Te Ching

ntermissions in a movie theater are mostly a relic in American cinema. That brief break in the middle of a captivating movie, when you can grab something from the snack bar, stretch your legs, or take a potty break, was something to look forward to years ago. These days, even the most bloated blockbuster requires moviegoers to sit still for the entire run.

In Bollywood cinema, where it is not uncommon for features to run over three hours, the intermission is still used, offering the luxury of pausing at the halfway point in a film. There is something delicious and freeing in the knowledge that, if you don't like the movie you are in, you can always sneak into another or walk right out the door into unknown adventures. More importantly, an intermission offers everyone in the theatre a time to pause and reflect. In some ways, that's how I was beginning to feel in my marriage.

Should I stay and stick it out, hoping the film miraculously gets better? Or should I embrace the fact that my marriage is no longer a movie I wish to star in and walk out the door into the great unknown, hoping to find (or create) a more enjoyable and fulfilling story for myself and my children?

The first home after my marriage in 1991 was a multi-generational home. It was common in India for sons to live with their parents and family as one large unit. Though the financial responsibility and big decisions were dependent on the son or head of household, the day-to-day management of the house and liaising between all family member needs were on the wife, in this case, me.

I came from a nuclear family. Back in my childhood home in Houston, our bedroom doors were always open. We casually shouted to gather everyone for dinner, and we all helped clean up afterward. Living in the joint home was a different world. We weren't allowed to make much noise. I had to keep my doors shut, so as not to disturb anyone with my singing. More days than not, I felt trapped, in desperate need of breathing room to think, create, and move without feeling like I was an unwelcome pest.

In 1993, while pregnant with Bhakti, I suggested to my husband that we move to our own home. With the addition of a newborn, I wanted a place we could call our own. My husband reacted poorly to this idea, relying on his usual episodes of emotional blackmail to talk me out of the idea of having a separate home for our growing family. This was a tactic of manipulation he had used from the very beginning of our marriage. Early on, I didn't know how to deal with it, but by this time, I had learned my own tactics to get what I wanted. Since having our own home was really about our child and her well-being, eventually he relented and, in 1994, three years into our marriage, we moved into a three-bedroom apartment we could afford. Most importantly for my husband, it was within walking distance of his family's house.

We moved once more, in 1996, and again right after my second daughter Sharayu was born in 2001. Thanks to the maturity of some financial instruments my father had assigned to my name years before, we had enough money build my dream house, a house that would have a purpose far beyond me or our family needs. In 2004, our home was featured in prestigious magazines and became a magnet for business events, dinners, and family gatherings that filled the calendar month after month. I had a wonderful staff, who were more like my family than hired help.

The house was my vision, and I felt a strong connection to every room, including the 1,500 square-foot dance space in the basement I designed, which was deemed the city's best, with wood floors, mirrored walls, a state-of-the-art music system, and a recording studio to film my students in their dance productions. My love for the outdoors was quenched by the hills and forest reserve to the back of the home and the exquisitely colorful and aromatic garden to the front, with its small ponds and water features. The meticulously planned infrastructure for recycling water, composting, and solar-powered heating exemplified my passion to care for the environment.

I poured everything I had into building that house, with a vision that it would be there for our daughters when we were long gone. This was my way to love and protect them beyond my lifetime. I hoped this beautifully designed home would help us, as a married couple, reconnect. In reality, it only created a lovely cocoon that enshrined us as our marriage continued to deteriorate.

Nearing Life's Intermission

In my mid-thirties, I experienced an intermission in my life. I surfaced briefly from my day-to-day identity as a wife, a role that had consumed me for over a decade. For the first time in a long time, I saw things clearly in the light of day.

Both motherhood and wifehood were, in many ways, thrust upon me. I probably would have chosen both at some point, but not as early as they were presented to me. While I embraced motherhood, wifehood remained empty, more of a title than an identity. Being a wife was all about the things I did, never about how I felt or what I thought or who I was. In 2006, at age thirty-four, I began to reckon with the spiritual and emotional toll my meaningless marriage was taking on me.

Not only did I play the role of wife within my home and family, but I was also responsible for cultivating and maintaining my public identity as the wife of a well-to-do businessman. My husband was from a prominent family, and he was personally ambitious. Certain expectations were thrust upon me that I couldn't avoid, such as supporting my husband's career, managing our household, and becoming a part of the city's social scene. Anything I could do to raise my profile in the community—and thus the family's profile—was highly encouraged.

My husband wasn't overbearing in day-to-day life. I largely had discretion over the parenting of our children and other family decisions, and I had the flexibility to do things like start and expand my dance studio. As long as my actions reflected well upon my husband and family, I was free to pursue my interests wherever they led, and they were leading me further afield all the time. In some ways, this was liberating.

As my dance studio expanded and diversified it became a gathering place for all people. Children, young adults, environmental groups, and a cross-section of industries were welcome. I was providing something valuable for people of all ages, and in the process amassing an incredible resource. Energy, enthusiasm, and community—all the ingredients for effective public service—were right there at my fingertips.

Our environmental work began with small projects, like introducing some of my dance students to concepts like recycling and renewable resources, and eventually, expanding into larger-scale versions of the kind of work I'd done in school and as a young woman. I went into the communities of Pune and offered basic public education about environmental concerns, a discernible problem in India—from the largest cities to the most remote villages—that I firmly believed could be resolved. I listened to people, tried my best to answer their questions, and brainstormed ways communities could become greener. With that information, I organized events for people to plant trees or separate trash from recyclables.

As it turned out, I wasn't the only person thinking about these things. Waste management is a huge business in India, as well as a significant policy concern. Eventually, my local projects attracted interest from the larger industry. Locally, I became known as a point person for green initiatives and environmental education. I was an increasingly visible figure in the city, and my husband could not have been happier. His father was a well-known social activist, and his family had put a lot of time, money, and advocacy into increasing access to clean water for villages.

My work dovetailed nicely with the family's interests and reputation in the community. As I learned, it was good to do good, but it was unequivocally better to be seen doing good. From the outside looking in, my life must have seemed idyllic. To the world, we were a smoothly functioning family, rising stars in the community, and an exemplar of a successful marriage. Privately, however, I struggled to come to terms with the limits of my life.

My innate drive, an almost insatiable capacity to work and achieve what my mind was set to do, was a gift that continuously led to great outcomes. Five hours of sleep at night and a ten-minute afternoon nap were all I need to be my energetic best. As the years passed and I spent more time on tasks that primarily benefited my husband, with little to no reciprocity or gratitude, I felt drained. In the depths of my being, I understood how my mother had felt years earlier when she expressed a strong desire for space to find her happiness.

Going into my marriage, I knew I was expected to play a large support role. I also knew I couldn't expect to instantly fall in love with my husband. However, knowing those things as a nineteen-year-old who had never been on a date was profoundly different from living that reality for over a decade. An arranged marriage isn't supposed to be loveless. Instead, love is expected to come eventually. The goal of a marriage is to create a durable partnership that can provide for and protect a family. I reminded myself of that often as the years went by and my husband and I failed to kindle any kind of romance between us.

Fear of imperfection and my lifelong need to please made me work harder than I should have to save a marriage neither one of us, from the very beginning, was interested in. Everything that was wrong, I considered a personal negative reflection on me. In the absence of romance, I tried my best to be a good friend to my husband. When I helped him with his work, when I took the household and child-rearing burdens off him, when I listened to his problems and tried to commiserate, I did it as a friend. I genuinely cared for him and wanted him to succeed. Many of the things I did I would do naturally for a dear friend. That is simply the core of my character.

The issue was my husband didn't seem interested in being a friend in return. Perhaps his understanding of friendship was different from mine. As in many cultures across the globe, women in India are frequently expected to shoulder the emotional and domestic burden in a relationship. Even by these standards, however, my marriage was asymmetrical. While he provided for us financially, he didn't support his wife or daughters emotionally. Much as my father had when I was a child, my husband devoted his whole self to his work. I believe he thought if he was successful there, he was being a good, successful husband and father.

Whenever I questioned whether we should remain married—something I did more and more frequently—I always assumed the failure of our marriage was my fault. Perhaps I hadn't given enough or made myself valuable enough. If I could just make my husband happier or provide more support, he would inevitably see how much I was trying to be a good wife to him. If I could solve all his problems, then he would finally see my needs were going unmet. Maybe then he would realize I needed time and attention too. Maybe he would finally see me as a worthy and equal partner, rather than a blend of a housekeeper, babysitter, and administrative assistant.

Shouldering the blame and responsibility for my unhappiness, I found new ways to help him with his work. My plan wasn't successful. Instead, it seemed to make things worse. It was as if my attention and care created a black hole within him that powerfully took everything in, including the light, and gave nothing back. The more I gave, the more he took. He needed so much from me, more every day, and I spent all my time trying to manage his life and his emotions. I felt like I was constantly trying to bridge the gap between the person he was and the person he wanted to be. The more he relied on me, the thinner I was stretched. As I gave him all I had, I was losing who I was and who I wanted to be. Meanwhile, all my efforts helped shape me into who he wanted me to be rather than growing me into the woman I wanted to become.

Death Threats and a Failed Attempt at Public Office

There was never one specific breaking point that marked the end, but rather a series of events stacked up like a game of Jenga that all came tumbling down. The most significant circumstance was my failed run for public office and the dangerous fallout afterwards.

Despite my highly visible and recognized work within the community, I was never particularly interested in politics. My husband, however, was convinced I should parlay my rising profile in the city to a seat on the local equivalent of a city council. He told me not to squander all the social capital I'd built through outreach. If I won, I would be responsible for managing several districts making up a large chunk of the city. It was a significant position, and I would need to campaign to get elected.

For him, my running for office was a matter of prestige and bragging rights with huge potential benefits—a rise in status and influence, not only for me but also for the family as a whole. He saw no significant downsides to being able to say, "My wife is a politician," which basically meant he would get a pass to do what he needed to do in his business.

Politics was a far cry from the dance studio or my other projects, and I probably wouldn't have pursued it if not for my husband's urging. I had spent so much time contorting into whatever shape and identity I thought would make him happy that, eventually, I started to think, *Maybe I am a politician. Maybe I can do this. If I try hard enough, I can make myself want this as much as he does. And then, maybe he'll love me and pay attention to me. Maybe we can finally be happy.*

For all the time I'd spent in the various communities in and around the city, I still wasn't familiar with the political scene in Pune. Crucially, I didn't realize how important these elections were for some people or how far they would go to improve their chances or keep the power they had accrued. As soon as my campaign gained traction, I began receiving threats of violence. Worse, the threats almost always targeted my daughters. It reached a boiling point when two men came to my door and told me, with eerie politeness, "Ma'am, you need to step down as a candidate or your children will be in danger."

With flashbacks of the attack that night at my parents' home all those years ago, I was terrified. Immediately, I told my husband I was dropping out of the race. To my shock, he calmly dismissed my fears and worries with a simple wave of his hand. "This happens all the time," he said. "No one's going to do anything. But just in case, we can get some security." His words reverberated within me like the peal of a bell.

Security? *Did I just hear him say that?* Thoughts of what happened the last time security was hired to protect me swirled through my mind. *No! Never again.* There was no way I would leave the safety of my daughters in the hands of a strange man disguised as a security guard.

My husband's passive and dismissive reaction to the death threats against our children shook me to my core. He saw the threats as small even inevitable nuisances that could easily be solved with money or power or both. It was clear to me that although he was the head of our family, and in theory ultimately responsible for our well-being, there were certain critical aspects of the world he simply didn't understand. Insulated by his wealth, by his family, and by his gender, nothing truly bad had ever happened to him, and so he quietly and naively assumed it never would.

He didn't know what it was like to be a girl or a woman in the world. To him, catcalls were normal, and he probably would have smiled or laughed if he ever received one. In his mind, my fear was overblown, and real violence was unlikely. It was confusing, to say the least. I was always so concerned with his feelings of security and comfort that I couldn't understand how he could be so dismissive of mine. Despite knowing what I had been through, he tried to convince me to stay in the race, but I didn't budge. A switch had flipped in my mind, and there was no going back on my decision. My husband was annoyed, surprised, and a bit confused. This was one of the first times I had offered serious resistance to something he wanted, and he didn't understand why. Although he did eventually accept my decision, something changed. The ground beneath us shifted, and I, at least, was suddenly rethinking everything I'd taken for granted for so long.

For years, I had devoted so much energy to my husband, to his sense of himself, to helping him reach his goals. In that process, I now realized,

I had become someone I didn't recognize and someone he no longer saw as being on his side. I was no longer a good wife. After all, a good wife would have yielded to his wishes and continued the campaign, putting aside her own fears about her children's safety. There was no way I could do that. How could anything that brought threats to our doorstep truly benefit Bhakti and Sharayu? Were all the things I was doing, inside the home and out, really making our family stronger or happier or safer? Most importantly, could I really trust my husband's judgment of what was best for all of us? I imagined all the different choices a good wife would have made.

Beneath these doubts and fears was an undeniable, bone-deep fatigue, like a constant, low-lying fog. I was tired, and I had been for so long that it had become part of my normal day. So much so that it took me a while to identify what I was experiencing. I was tired in my body, in my mind, and in my soul. For more than ten years, I hadn't really nourished any part of myself. I was pouring out my care, my energy, my time, and my love, and no one, including me, was putting anything back in. Now, a decade and a half into my marriage, I was emotionally and energetically hollow.

In response to this emptiness, my body and mind went into self-preservation mode. Out of necessity, I started to slowly take a step back from nearly everything I was doing. I suspended my dance company, reduced my community work, let go of most social commitments, and tried to do something I hadn't done in a long time: focus on myself. At first, it was like trying to speak a language I hadn't used since childhood. I needed to be reacquainted with everything I knew and liked about myself. Over the course of many months, I finally rediscovered who I really was and who I had been all along.

Outside Attention, Outside Attraction

With my dance studio back in operation, I resumed my world travels, serving as a kind of ambassador for India's modern dance community.

I performed in Europe and in the US, leading dance-therapy workshops for individuals and groups. Once again, my career path kept leading me to the corporate world, as I provided workshops for companies as employee enrichment. I suppose you can't escape your destiny.

Taking great joy in this work, I was gratified to see I was making a difference in the lives of others. It allowed me to appreciate myself for who I was, not for who my parents or my husband or my children wanted me to be, not as I had to be, but as my truest self. Finding her was like peeling away a thousand fragile layers of an onion to reveal what had always been there at the heart of me.

As I learned more about myself, I experienced the first real romantic connection of my life. During my travels for dance, I crossed paths with a man who was a revolutionary presence in my life. I had never dated, and love was still a mystery to me. I knew what care and compassion felt like since that's how I loved everyone around me. I knew how to give love but didn't know how to receive it. Unsure how to be loved by a man, what it would feel like, or how to accept it, I envisioned what a good partner for me would be and how I would be for him. This dear friend liked me, and he was very frank about it. It wasn't a sexualized liking either.

He admired me. He thought my dancing was beautiful and I was talented, and he wanted to know more about what I thought and felt and wanted from the world. No one had ever questioned me about these aspects of life. Being with him was like a breath of fresh air. I felt rejuvenated at the thought that someone might genuinely be interested in me.

Over time, we became friends, and shortly thereafter, our relationship began to morph into something else, not quite friendship and not quite romance. Despite having been married for more than fifteen years, I was unpracticed at managing romantic relationships. When I think now about what I felt for him, I think mostly of an overwhelming sense of hope. He was the first person to really make me feel there might be someone in the world who could love me, the woman I was becoming.

Deepening my relationship with this man felt like grabbing on to a life preserver in the middle of stormy seas. Having someone, him in particular, rescue me felt good, but not in a physically intimate way. The people closest to me—my own family and in-laws—seemed to ignore me or refuse to acknowledge me, no matter what good I did in my community work or within the family. Because of that, and quite unplanned, I was open to receive validation from other sources. I had a deep, unmet yearning for authentic appreciation, respect, and love.

My relationship with this man wasn't the only reason I decided to accelerate the process of separation I'd begun, but it was *a* reason. Mostly, as I began to feel more and more confident being myself without caveats or apologies, I was less willing to force myself to live in a way that felt inauthentic. I wanted to explore the woman I was, and I was afraid that if I kept going through the motions of wifehood, I would wind up trapped by that ill-fitting role.

As I began to spread my wings and transform into a new version of myself, I saw an irony in the work I loved. As I sought to empower kids and women around me, encouraging them to never settle, to focus on their strengths, to go out into the world and live their freedom, I had been doing just the opposite. Again and again, I told the girls I taught about the importance of love, how they deserved to feel loved and cherished, but I had simply accepted a relationship in which all the kindness and consideration went in only one direction, like water flowing downhill.

Dearest Daughters

Life is in its momentum. Things are in motion with your career and your heart . . . and you're headed in the direction you envisioned with full vigor, strength, and confidence. Look at you! You are leading yourself, passing all kinds of tests, and maturing more each day. I'm so proud of you.

I love the way you laugh and find ways to keep everyone together and happy. Even the young minds and kids around you. Boy, can they open your eyes to realities, especially of not being their age anymore.

It's been a long time, dear. You feel like you are finally in the center and getting a hint of peace and satisfaction. You know that feeling when you throw pebbles into the ocean and they dance around until they find their spot on the sea floor? It's a bit like that, huh?

But can I ask you something? Is this really what you chose? Or—and I dare ask out of my love for you—have you allowed it to be chosen for you? My fear is sometimes, without realizing it, you might be set-tling. It's comfortable and easy, and there's a chance for you to kind of get lazy in it too. I get it.

My dears, how many times did you allow people or things to chose over you? Why were you okay to overlook a few things and discount you in the interest of harmony? But the notes of a harmony include you too. I pray you are happy, but I can't help but wonder if you really are. Settling feels peaceful, but actually, it is a compromise. Your sense of love, in reality, feels lonely. That's not love, my dears. Love rejoices in the center and lives dynamically in balance, not in settling.

I say to you, "It's your turn! Keep it there!" It's okay to expand and discover how you are maturing. Ask why you like or dislike certain things, what excites you, and where you need to put boundaries for your balance, your center. It might feel like a tornado since you are opening your eyes within to more of the untapped you.

Remember the tricky part, balance is always moving. Love loves to dance around, but with everything constantly changing, including you, it's only natural that you have to keep up. So gather all that is around you and feel. Feel, my dears. Open you heart, let Love speak in the middle of it all. Yes, Love is like a moving target. Even still, feel the center, its balance. And then, from your center, feel the expanse. I can already see you making a difference for you and others. Your legacy is taking root in the stability of your center. Because even though you may not know exactly what you want, you are aware, and you respectfully know what you don't.

Love always,
Rani

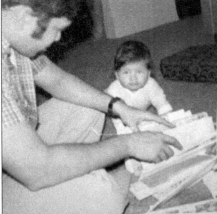

"Can I help organize?"
Baba and me.
Houston, TX, 1972 ↑

Mom and me, always in style.
Houston, TX, 1977 ↑

Baba and me.
Houston, TX, 2021 ↑

Mom and me. Teacher-student interchanges with music.
Pune, India, 2021 ↑

Interning at Worldwide Oilfield Machine.
Houston, TX, 1986
→

With WOM team
members.
Houston, TX, 2022
←

My Aaji and me as an infant.
Thane, India, 1972 ↑

Baba, Mom, and me.
Canemont, Worldwide Oilfield Machine,
Houston, TX, 2021 ↑

Baba, Mom, and me.
South Main, Worldwide Oilfield Machine,
Houston, TX, 1986 ↑

With my girls, Sharayu, two years old
and Bhakti, nine years old.
Pune, India, 2002 →

"Hear no evil, speak no evil, see no evil."
With my girls, Sharayu and Bhakti.
New York, NY, 2022 ↓

Dance days with ISHA.
Pune, India, 2006 ↑

Dance venue.
Dubai, UAE, 2022 →

Blacksmith forging.
Waco, Texas, 2019
←

My brother Mahesh with nieces and nephews.
Jadhavgadh, India, 2017
↓

Sailing with my girls.
Mallorca, Spain, 2019 ↑

At the MS 150 finish line.
Austin, TX, 2014
↑

Impact India.
Pune, India, 2017
←

Vision International students.
Pune, India, 2022
→

Homer Garza, known as
Daddy Homer, with my
Baba.
Sugar Land, TX, 2021
←

Three generations of Puranik women.
My daughters Sharayu and Bhakti
with Mom and me.
Houston, TX, 2022
←

Celebrating light, love, and legacy with
Bhakti and Sharayu.
Houston, TX, 2017
→

Chapter Six:

WHEN I BECAME A WOMAN
THIRTY-FIVE TO FORTY-TWO YEARS OLD

Darkness cannot drive out darkness; only light can do that.
~ Martin Luther King Jr.

N o one leaves a place, a situation, or an identity all at once. We exit in parts, in pieces. Often, the process of leaving begins within. Like water evaporating a little at a time, leaving is an invisible yet very real phenomenon through which your mind slowly begins the process of detaching. Time and the process unravel who you are, and *whose* you are, until one day, like magic, your old identity simply disappears.

Gradually, I had vanished from my marriage. My heart no longer felt like that of a wife. This internal shift was so significant that, at times, the wife I had become appeared as a lost and dark face gazing back at me in the mirror. Who was this woman? Why was she here? Where had I gone?

Feeling trapped in an unhappy marriage was like being the star of a choreographed rhythm of movements. For the audience, it was a vision of grace and beauty, but for the performer, it was an over-rehearsed flow of motions to reach the coda of the grand pas de deux, the end of the ballet performance. Watching the dancer, the audience does not realize the pain she's endured perfecting her craft, the aches in her limbs, the damage to her feet. They see only her graceful, elegant movements and her emotionless face, never focusing on what's stirring in her eyes.

Dancing was a core medium of my expression. It was as sacred to me as the sanctity of marriage. Both were also enigmatic, masking truths, with interpretations left to the audience. In my marriage, the audience was my husband, who was right next to me every day and saw only what he wanted to see, oblivious to what was really there. Most times, he saw only himself in the performance.

The emptiness I felt when trying to discuss my needs with my husband left an ache within me. I was never able to get through to him. He heard my words, and at times reacted in a vaguely agreeable manner. However, the cultural traditions—or perhaps his own beliefs and thought patterns—never allowed for a change in his behavior. Over time, and over many failed attempts at communication, all my efforts felt pointless. Each conversation seemed to evaporate into thin air as soon as the words left my mouth.

My final attempt at communication was presented in the form of dance, always my emotional refuge. I believed I could convey my position through movement without him feeling attacked or disrespected. If I could show him how I felt through my art, he would see how profoundly unhappy I was. Perhaps then he would understand.

One evening, I pulled my husband away from the evening news and begged him to come to my studio to watch the routine I had painstakingly spent several weeks choreographing. He unwillingly followed me to the studio and watched, his eyes fixed on me, devoid of emotion throughout the entire performance. Upon finishing, I stood in silence, slightly out of breath, nervously gazing at him, searching his face, hoping for some emotion or response. There was none. He didn't utter a single word. He didn't clap or smile; his demeanor remained the same, emotionless. I should have known how futile it would be.

After a minute that seemed like an hour, he stood up, turned away, and walked out of the room. Still frozen, awaiting a response of understanding, I heard the television volume rise from upstairs. He had gone back to watching the evening news. Like a young dancer auditioning before a panel of judges whose closing words are "Next," I felt foolish. I thought this was the performance of a lifetime. My judge was unimpressed.

Defeated, empty, and broken, I sat on the floor and sobbed, realizing something within me had monumentally shifted. This would be my final outpouring of tears in this situation. My emotional waters evaporated rapidly. The detachment accelerated, and my core became quiet. From then on, our conversations were reduced to small talk and logistics, brief updates about the children, and minimal chatter to stave off the silence. I believe he accepted our conversations as indication that the problem had gone away and I had acquiesced into our familiar pattern. What he didn't realize was that I had already begun to shut the door to this part of my life. I had danced my finale.

As I began to mentally leave wifehood, I noticed something incredible: after thirty-five years of life as a female, I was finally starting to become a woman. That meant finally living my life for me, thinking of what I wanted, what I was good at, and what I felt called to. For the first time in my life, my initial concern wasn't about what anyone else thought; it was about what would make me genuinely happy.

The Finale: Finding My Air

For years, my consistent message to my students was: "Find your air, your breath, your freedom, your life. Be who you are. Build on your strengths. Respectfully let go of what does not serve you." It was all good, solid advice, but I'd never adopted it in my own life, until now.

Married for sixteen years and conditioned to deny my own voice, I had been too scared to heed my own advice. Deep inside, I was gasping for air. Time was up. I just couldn't pretend anymore. From the outside looking in, my life was still picture perfect. However, internally, I was exhausted and depleted. I had given all I had and created all I could create. I didn't want to break tradition, but it was unavoidably time to move on.

Asking permission to be free without hurting anyone was next to impossible. My mind swirled with the uncertainties and fear of being judged as ungrateful and selfish. How would I manage after I left? How would I care for my girls? What was my plan? I didn't have all the answers, and I didn't know what I wanted. I knew what I didn't want, and that was enough.

I chartered unknown waters when I got married. Now, I was making a decision to move into another unknown. This time, I was making the decision to do it for myself. Communicating with my husband continued to be a struggle. He barely registered that anything was wrong or different between us. Finally, in January 2007, I approached him and said, "I need to be away from you." I told him I wanted to go to Houston with the girls and take time to collect my thoughts.

It was a big step, but I didn't consider it to be the most extreme option. After all, my parents had frequently lived apart, either for logistical or personal reasons, and it had always seemed like a way to get space without completely severing the connection. In my mind, as long as our daughters were taken care of and safe with me, this arrangement could work.

What my husband heard was something completely different. His interpretation was that I was leaving him, having an affair, or having a mental breakdown. More so, he heard that I wanted to run away with *his* kids. He had an image to protect, and any action that would expose him to judgment or hurt his standing in the community was intolerable.

He hated the thought of opening our personal problems to scrutiny from outsiders. It was already bad enough that I'd dropped out of the local political race. For me to move to another country would mean utter humiliation to him. The appearance of a less than successful and happy family awoke a fury in him that I hadn't expected.

He refused to allow me to leave India, threatening to hurt himself if I left. This was his emotional blackmail of choice, which he had used many times over the years. Calmly, I called his bluff. "If this is the path you choose, then by all means, do it."

Regardless of the concessions I offered, he found a way to punish me. If I suggested getting an apartment for a trial separation, he claimed it was so I could see someone else. If I pushed for a full, legal divorce and wanted primary custody of the girls, he claimed I was being selfish and only wanted to turn them against him. If I agreed to his custody terms, he claimed I did not care about my children. In the court of opinion, I would lose either way. I agreed to forfeit my claim to most of my personal and marital assets, including my thoughtfully designed and purpose-filled home, which should have been a nest for our children's future. Even that wasn't enough for him. I was on trial in Wonderland, where nothing made sense and the rules constantly changed as we tumbled down an emotional rabbit hole.

Despite everything, I pushed forward. In March 2007, I consulted a divorce attorney, and soon thereafter, I handed my husband the divorce papers. He took them from my hands, tore them up in front of my face, and threw them into the air. In shock and disbelief, I stood frozen. Our interactions had become toxic, both in front of our daughters and in private. My mom visiting our home and witnessing the struggle and repercussions marked a turning point. She simply said to me, "You can't do this anymore." She, more than anyone else, knew how much I wanted the marriage to work; however, the time had come to be realistic about my expectations. My girls and I were in an unhealthy environment.

Knowing I needed to lead by example with my actions, I had to make some difficult decisions.

I began with a conversation with Bhakti. I went into her room, where she was studying with a smile, as always. For a brief moment, I thought, *No wonder her pet name, Khushi, meaning happiness, stuck to her throughout the years. She always has a pleasant and kind disposition, no matter the situation.* Pausing the music playing on her Walkman, she removed her headset, looked at me, and chirped, "What's up, Ma?"

There was a long pause as I approached her, silence, as I sat next to her. She gazed at me, waiting for me to say what was on my mind. Ashamed to look her in the eye, yet assertive in my decision, I uttered, "Khushi, I need to separate from your dad."

Without skipping a beat, she blurted out, "About time!"

My eyes lifted to meet hers. With a surprised tilt of my head, I asked, "Really? You knew?"

Her answer is living proof that children are much more intelligent and intuitive than parents give them credit for. "Of course, Ma. I knew," she said.

With that, I felt confident to take the next step with Bhakti, which was to move forward with plans for her to attend boarding school, as I had in ninth grade. The timing was ideal so she could be away from the ongoing tension and drama at home.

Sharayu was younger, only six years old at the time, and I was concerned the impending change would be more difficult for her. I couldn't bring myself to send her that far away from me. My husband, quite aware the girls were my number one priority, and in some ways my Achilles heel, knew this was where he could inflict injury. He began a campaign to attack me through what he knew I loved most, my daughters.

After I moved out of our house and into our old apartment, fifteen minutes away, he filed for restitution, which meant I was basically under house arrest. I was not permitted to leave the country. He then refused to let me see my younger daughter, as a form of punishment. However, nothing could keep me away from her. With the help of our home staff, I saw her each day. They met me halfway between our homes so we could spend time together. Most of the time, I would meet her at the park, where we played and talked about her day and homework. Although not ideal, the arrangement allowed me to keep my lioness eyes on her to make sure she was safe and taken care of during this unprecedented storm in our lives.

One day, I decided to bring Sharayu back to my apartment so we could have time in the comfort of home. I greatly underestimated how vengeful and calculating my husband had become. Within minutes, police were banging on my door, forcing me to return her to his house immediately. One thing did catch my attention; this time they were all women officers.

Hoping to appeal to their femaleness, I asked, "Is all of this necessary?"

Sympathetically, one officer replied, "Madam, we are so sorry, but we are not in a position to say anything."

Sharayu looked at me with the bravest eyes I had ever seen from a tiny, innocent person, and we went downstairs together, followed by the officers. I told them I would drop her home. They were fine with that. Parked in front of "her" house, she kissed me and said, "Mom, we will be okay. I'll see you soon. I love you." My heart sank, but my eyes showed a smile to her. I had to remain confident and calm.

For almost a year, I lived in the apartment, under these conditions, constantly struggling to see my child. My husband's family, made the ordeal even more complex, using their business and political connections to portray me as an unfit mother who didn't love her children or her husband, and who was involved in an affair. All this was untrue. I was up against a tough fight.

When a long-term relationship ends, there is often a scramble to divide loyalties amongst friends, acquaintances, and even extended family. For my husband and me, that happened in an extreme fashion. If he couldn't keep our problems out of the public eye entirely, he was determined to make sure the narrative everyone heard favored him as much as possible. Whenever some element of our divorce became public knowledge, he went out of his way to portray me in a negative light. Eventually, some of his family retreated from their slanderous behavior, although they hoped I would rethink the divorce. They rightfully viewed his approach and behavior as only worsening the situation.

The longer the divorce dragged on, the uglier it became, and the more the people around us wanted nothing to do with this terrible situation. They no longer cared who was right or wrong; they just wanted it all to go away. In fact, most of our mutual acquaintances decided to keep their distance and let us work out our situation without their intervention. What that meant, practically speaking, was that I was very much alone. No one was going to step in and rescue me from this seemingly inescapable crisis, just like no one had rescued me from walking down the aisle in the first place. I had to find my own way out, and it certainly wasn't easy. It was one of the most painful episodes I had ever experienced.

With very few weapons at my disposal—culturally, legally, or financially—I learned my best chance at success was to concede whenever I could. After all, he had most of the power in our marriage and was not afraid to use it. To emotionally appease him, I agreed our marital problems were my fault, reassuring him that he was a good person who had tried his best and that he was blameless. I conceded financially, agreeing not to pursue any spousal or child support, and gave him all our marital assets.

I honored his desire to keep things private, even when he blatantly chose not to do the same. I spent so much time accommodating him, looking for the magic combination that would make him accept our divorce, that I didn't notice how serious or how dangerous the situation had become. I wanted to believe my husband would inevitably accept the divorce and let me leave in peace. After all, I was determined to go, so he couldn't keep me prisoner. I learned the hard way that you never really know a person until you go into battle either with them or against them.

My husband was willing to go much farther to get what he wanted than I'd ever imagined. He hired men to follow me when I moved out of our home. It was not the first time I'd felt a sense of physical danger, but it convinced me my only real chance to get away was to put an ocean between us. I had spent much of my adult life in India, but it was time to return to Houston, my home, where I had family to love and support me. Unfortunately, going back to America proved more difficult than I imagined.

Surprisingly, my husband made it clear, time and time again, that the endless maze of financial ruin, legal intimidation, and personal attacks would end the moment I dropped the divorce and moved back in with him. This is not to say that he would have forgiven me quickly or even at all. Had I returned home, I'm sure I would have spent a long time paying for my perceived transgressions, but he would have me back and my life could be "normal" again. That identity of being a wife was waiting for me, enveloping and suffocating as it was, but safe and secure by his definition. Although I was ashamed and felt like a failure, I couldn't go back. I had to speak up and stand up for myself. I had already left him in the ways that mattered most. He was trying to breathe life into a dead thing.

In March 2008, a full year after I'd filed for divorce, I made a trip to visit Mom at the school she had founded and grown in the mountains of India. As soon as she saw me, my withdrawn and thin face and how much weight I'd lost amidst the turmoil, she immediately knew what was on my mind and in my heart. There was no need to say much. Mom understood and offered sympathy, but little advice. She was saddened to see I wasn't happy in my marriage, but she wasn't completely surprised; it had been clear to her for many years.

Her own marriage had been difficult, and she knew the sense of being squeezed into a role that no longer fit. The intensity of my husband's response to my departure, however, shocked her. After all, she and my father separated amicably and still supported one another. After many years of living apart, they grew as great friends who respected each other and gave each other space. They were divorced in all but the legal sense, and it happened without any major bitterness or spite. Understanding the urgency of my need to be free, she gave me her blessing, $200 cash, and a plane ticket to Houston.

I had another major obstacle to overcome. I had no status in the US because I'd surrendered my residency years earlier at my husband's request. He had also taken my passport and drained my bank accounts. I had no money to my name. In order to escape and chart a new course, I had to make drastic and painful choices no mother should ever have to make. I would need to leave India without my beloved daughters. I would then have to acquire the appropriate documents and establish my life again in the US before getting my girls back. The lioness had to separate from her young cubs. It was unnatural.

Leaving my girls behind was the hardest decision I've ever made in my life, but I knew I had no choice. I was thirty-six years old. I had arrived at my life's intermission. Halfway through the movie, I'd seen enough to guess how the rest would unfold. Without movement, there would be no happy ending for anyone in this story. I could either continue to sit there in the darkened theater, staring up at the screen and hoping some miraculous plot twist would suddenly make things better, or I could stand up and leave. The time had come for me to go out into the world and fight with my last breath to create a better future for myself and get my daughters back.

The Longest Goodbye

A month later, a week before my departure, I went to visit Bhakti in boarding school. I had to see her before I left. I needed to know she understood something of what was happening so she wouldn't mistake my leaving for abandonment. That would have broken my heart.

"Bhakti, Grandma has given me a ticket to Houston, and I am going to go," I told her. "I don't know when I'm coming back, because I have no idea what my position is going to be. I've tried staying here for a year, and it is just getting worse and worse for everybody." This was such an adult circumstance. I hoped her teenage mind could comprehend.

At fourteen years of age, and wise beyond her years, she looked at me knowingly and said, "Okay, Mom, you go. I will miss you. Keep in touch with me." I gave her a mobile phone, a forbidden item at that time in the dorms, and we promised we would talk whenever we could.

Sharayu was only seven and much too young to fully understand what was happening. I didn't know how to explain to her that I was leaving her father, not abandoning her, and I needed to be in a safe place while I figured things out. Thankfully, she had her school routine and two best friends, and our staff was sympathetic to my cause. For their own good, I did not tell them what I had planned, instead telling them I was leaving for a long dance tour. That way, if they were asked my whereabouts, they could answer truthfully that they were not aware I'd gone to Houston. I gave them enough money to take care of Sharayu's needs and prayed we'd all be okay.

On my last day in India, I snuck back into my house. Both dogs gave me a huge welcome, and Tara, the golden-brown ten-year-old, kept whining for me to continue petting her. I went through the kitchen, where the cook was busy preparing something delicious, and made my way upstairs to the drawers that held my American clothes. I smiled inside as I took a final look at the bedroom wall. Upon it hung three hand-drawn cartoon character sketches of me and both girls made by an artist during our trip to Venice, Italy, a couple years back.

Seated atop the bed, I flipped through our photo albums, wishing I could bring them with me, but there was not space for all those memories in my one bag. So I left them all, believing we would someday make new memories together. After completing my sparse packing with robot-like motions, I stood in the center of the room. I wanted to cry for what I was leaving behind, but my tears had run dry. This was my decision point. I was ready for what was next in my life.

At four o'clock in the afternoon, Sharayu was watching one of her favorite cartoons in the living room. Sitting next to her, I tried to enjoy our last few moments together without alerting her that anything was different. The taxi would come at any minute. My heart ached knowing I would be leaving her behind.

My husband made it clear that he intended to do whatever was necessary to keep Sharayu from me. He could do it too. Even if he had been willing to give me full custody, I would have had difficulty bringing the girls to the US, given my visitor's visa and uncertain plans for work and citizenship. I spent many nights sleepless and anxious, fearing that if I left India, I would be abandoning my girls, especially Sharayu. I knew they would be physically safe with their father, but I'd always tried to ensure they didn't experience the loneliness and isolation that had characterized my own childhood.

From the kitchen, the kind cook asked in a sing-song tone, "Miss Rani, what do you want for dinner today?"

That's when it hit me hard. I was leaving. I didn't have an answer to his question. As my heart raced and my cheeks flushed, I took a deep breath and answered, "You can choose. Just see what Sharayu wants and make something for her."

Moments later, the taxi arrived. My time was up. I gave my sweet daughter a kiss on her forehead and said, "I have to go on a dance tour."

I traveled now and then, so it wasn't unusual for me to be gone for a few days. I always came back. Always. Until now.

She nodded and continued watching her show.

I said, "I will be back soon, so you have fun and don't worry about me. I'll call you when I can."

She was so used to this routine that she didn't even remove her eyes from the screen. "Okay, Mom," she said. With that, and a small nod of thanks to the cook, I left.

As I opened the taxi door, a light wind blew across my face, and I recalled a memory from childhood. I had rushed out the door to catch my school bus. As I took a seat and caught my breath, I realized I'd forgotten my lunch. I was in charge of making lunch for myself and my siblings every morning, carefully choosing their favorite ingredients for sandwiches and snacks. I even drew cartoons with a special message to liven up the dull brown lunch bags. I always made sure they had their brown bags, but that day, I would have to go hungry until I got home later after school.

When I returned home hungry with a sulky expression, my grandmother was waiting for me. She lovingly handed me a sandwich and gave me advice, which became a guiding force in my life. "*Rani, pudhe zayachya adhi, ek kshan mage valun bagh.*" Before you go anywhere, she'd advised me, take a quick second to glance behind. Confirm within where you are going. Make sure you've taken everything you need, and if you leave something behind, you will do so knowingly.

I needed that reminder now, more than ever. Although I knew Sharayu was in good hands with my family-like staff and friends, the overwhelming pain in my heart quickened. It was unquestionably the most profound hurt I had ever experienced. As I sat in the taxi, driving away from home, from Sharayu, air escaped my lungs and I found it difficult to breathe. Full of guilt in that moment, I had to remember to love myself and seek self-respect. I had to walk my talk of trusting who

I am and giving myself grace, even in the midst of indescribable pain. As the taxi gained speed, I begged God for a little mercy and glanced behind, one last time, at the life I chose to leave.

One of the most difficult things I have done in my adult life was getting on that plane and leaving my daughters. At my core was the faith that my decision to leave would eventually result in a favorable outcome for us all. As I was learning to like myself, I was also learning to trust myself, and with that trust came the strength to move forward despite fear. Trusting my abilities as a mother, and standing in the independence and inner strength I had cultivated in my girls, gave me the confidence of a lioness. My years of watchfulness, letting them struggle and learn through great challenges, had led me to this moment to withdraw and let them stand on their own. I knew they were strong enough and prepared to weather this storm.

Starting Over in America

Getting to America felt like stepping out of a stifling room and taking a big lungful of cool air on a crisp fall day. Unfortunately, it was far from my final step on my transformative journey, as both my children were still in India. I may have been shucking the role of wife, but motherhood was in my bones. I needed Bhakti and Sharayu with me, and they needed me as well.

My soon-to-be ex-husband was a loving father and showed it more through the language of gifts than emotional connection. He worked long hours and prioritized his actions based on how they impacted the family financially. My children were physically secure with him, but they needed a certain kind of mental attention he just wasn't equipped to give. Although friends, family, and the house staff stepped in where they could, it just wasn't the same. Sometimes, children just need their mother.

Additionally, as happens in many ugly divorces, he began to see the girls as yet another potential weapon, rather than as small, vulnerable people in need of love and attention during an uncertain time in their lives. He wanted to win, whatever that meant for him. Mostly, I think he wanted to make leaving more difficult for me, but he had no concern for how his actions would impact the girls.

Bhakti was nearly a teenager when our divorce began. Her father saw her as already too fully formed and something of a lost cause in terms of building an allyship with him. He considered her too much like me and too sympathetic to my side of the conflict. As a consequence, our younger daughter, Sharayu, became the bargaining tool between the two of us. In her, he saw a chance to be more intimately involved in the rearing of a child and to mold her more actively than he had Bhakti. Sharayu could still be "his" in the way he thought of Bhakti as "mine."

Through some absurd math, he calculated that each parent should get one child, which somehow was an acceptable solution for everyone but me. I worried because one of society's flaws is the tendency to think of people, especially children, as props rather than complex beings with needs of their own. For some, having a child can be more about a title or role and less about having an emotional connection.

By the time I landed in Texas, I was too busy for fear. I had to build a whole new life, and I had to do it quickly. Upon arriving, I went home to be with my father. In another time, I might have been afraid to show up at his door with the disgrace of a divorce looming over me. But as a woman and mother on a mission, I was no more willing to change my life to gain my father's approval than I had been willing to change to suit my husband. I was pleasantly surprised by his response to me.

Like my mother, he was not happy to know I had left my husband. He would have preferred we resolved our marital problems. After all, he liked my husband because he was a dedicated worker and successful in his career. But that didn't change his fundamental fatherly impulses toward me. As my legal troubles stretched on (and on, and on, and on), my father began to understand my motivations more. Although he was silent early on, over time he saw my soon-to-be ex-husband lacked several of the qualities of a good partner and caregiver. I honestly wasn't banking on Dad providing me anything besides a place to stay for a few days, but he welcomed me and accepted my choices. He was very supportive, and I was appreciative.

Working in the Family Business

Getting a job was one of my first priorities when I arrived in America. With only a visitor's visa, there were legal restrictions regarding my ability to work. I would have worked the drive-thru at McDonald's if I'd needed to, but my father agreed to sponsor me for my work visa (and later my residency), so I rejoined the Worldwide Oilfield Machine (WOM) family.

I had worked at WOM before I got married, and like muscle memory, it felt natural to return. Back in 1991, right before my wedding, my dad had told my prospective in-laws, "I can say one thing for sure. You are taking my right hand, my greatest gift." I had no intentions of being a right hand when I rejoined the company, but I wanted to be a meaningful helping hand. And just like that, I was in the position my father had anticipated for me when I went off to college. I was finally part of the family business.

Dad is a true garage-to-globe success story. His company, WOM, started with a spark of an idea, which he passionately grew to a flaming torch. WOM launched when I was two years old, after my father developed a special metal-coating process called integrated hardfacing. This extended the life of a base metal, allowing it to withstand harsh environments of high temperature and pressure in the oil patch. The technique is an art which requires diligence to find the perfect blend between metal, heat, fusing, and cooling. Then, obtaining a metal-to-metal seal with a mirror finish tied it all in perfection, making it the essential heart of every valve WOM made.

After he finished working at his primary job, my father had worked late into the evenings in a rented garage, developing these special processes only he had expertise in. My mother and I would visit him with dinner. Later, I would fall asleep on the floor in the makeshift pantry while my mom patiently accompanied him during long nights as he perfected technical details.

As the business grew, I grew up alongside it. By the time I was twelve, my summers were spent at WOM, in a three-room building with a buzzing workshop. Copy machines were fairly new, and I occasionally made copies of my hands and arms. Friday after-school visits were common. My mother and I always had weekend filing and work projects for which we packed cardboard boxes with manila folders and invoices, documents, purchase orders, and bills, all needing to be filed. Back in those days, we had three-fold copies with carbon paper in between each sheet, which left a strange blue residue on the tips of my fingers with every sheet I touched. I became a filing machine in no time.

Dad knew I was organized, so I spent hours filing paperwork and creating systems to organize his office, including a labeling process to track inventory. When I look back, I see my close association to processes, internal structures, inventory, and finance. From my earliest childhood memories, I realized I'm naturally a very fast worker. Once I'm given a task, I find ways of speeding it up. Dad would give me a task and expect me to be done in a week. I would finish in three hours. He would check my work and note that I always went above and beyond. I would not only answer the questions he asked me; I anticipated his next requests and had ready answers to those as well. If he asked me to do research, I did, and I would provide proof of my answers. That's when he realized my capacity and potential at the company.

When I was sixteen, WOM's flagship building settled on three acres. I drove forklifts, filed checks, and knew everyone in the shop. Dad treated people with respect and worked with them shoulder to shoulder. Product innovation and excellence were his passions. WOM was making a name all over the globe. At 3:00 a.m., fax machines buzzed at home. I would hear the ding and rush to watch the thermal paper glide through this new technology.

When I was seventeen, WOM in India was established, and within one year, a building was constructed. I was on the team that planted the very first row of coconut trees on the premises. Over the next seventeen years, although I was not a direct part of the business, I heard his stories of achievement. Dad ventured successfully into five countries, bought out partners, and always gave God credit for his blessings. He was and continues to be a humble man, who sees the best in all people and treats all with dignity and respect.

When I returned to the company in my mid-thirties, WOM had grown exponentially. The small torch was now an awe-inspiring Olympic one. Although some things were familiar, much had changed. Dad's drive was focused on the future and on production. He had a quiet, non-intrusive demeanor around the office. Consequently, people sometimes took advantage of his kind, non-confrontational nature.

A handful of people became leads who reported to him and informed him of what he wanted to hear, not necessarily the truth of what was really going on. To the company, nothing was more important than moving forward, but no one bothered to look at the cost. Checks and balances were not a priority. Verifying and assuring due process tended to get in the way of getting things done, so these integral parts of running a healthy business were quickly undermined.

I naturally gravitated toward human resources and personnel development, building processes and systems that allowed people to work together more effectively. I didn't just want to work at my father's company because it was easy or convenient; I wanted to add value. Over time, people, including my father, started to appreciate and depend upon my efforts.

In my personal life, I explored a more serious relationship with the man I'd met through my dancing. It quickly became clear to me that I needed him during that time in my life because I had never really had a chance to explore other connections. I had gone almost directly from high school to marriage, with no space in between for freedom, mistakes, and discovery. He helped me recover that part of myself, and through our relationship, I started to believe I deserved to be loved. Whether consciously or not, I had envisioned marriage as a relationship between two people more or less like co-workers with a shared set of obligations. Fun, joy, lightness, and friendship were things I didn't even realize I was missing until they were in front of me.

Finding a Deeper Faith

In addition to going on a personal and professional search in Houston, I also started exploring my spirituality again after years of not thinking deeply about such matters. All my life, I had been searching in one way or another, and I'd often found what I believed were pieces of my personal puzzle: Krishna, dance, the elements, traditional Hinduism. All these things offered me some of what I needed, but never a completeness. I always believed in a higher power, something greater than all of us, which allows the sun to rise and our hearts to beat. But I never felt wholly comfortable or complete.

In the States, I actively studied various religions, trying to discover what I had missed and was still lacking. I tried to understand myself, and that meant finding out why I existed, what life was truly for. I had left behind so much when I stepped away from being a wife. The revelation that I now had nearly infinite options was exhilarating and a little scary. I wanted to try everything, to wear every way of being like a fashion montage in a romantic movie.

At first, I dug deep into Buddhism, but found I had an internal struggle with one of the bedrock tenets of that faith: pain is inevitable. Buddhism teaches that life is like a rising wave that inevitably must fall, and we need to move with it, to abandon caring and need. Underneath that wave is the inescapable pain that humans have to live through. I'd had enough suffering. I couldn't live with a belief system that built everything on a foundation of pain. I had to move toward a different model, one that didn't centralize the misery of life in that way.

I then explored Taoism, which offers a great sense of freedom. The world sort of washes over you, and you become a bit of flotsam, going along with it. Taoism was helpful for a certain period in my life because I felt as though I'd finally freed myself from life's moorings and I was learning to sail my ship. Taoism is about "flow," and I was attracted to that idea, so I just trusted everything would be fine and flow like a river. Eventually, however, I began to crave a destination. I didn't like the ambivalence, the calm unknowing. If all we could do was go with the flow, who set the tides in motion? Why did we float along? There had to be something more.

One fateful day in 2008, I awoke ready for a day of relaxation. As I flipped through the TV channels, a familiar face caught my attention. It was someone I used to watch on Sundays when I still lived in Pune, during the separation and ensuing divorce. The running scroll on the bottom of the screen read "Lakewood Church in Houston, Texas." That's when it dawned on me. *I'm in Houston. I need to check this out in person!*

It happened to be Easter Sunday, and the next service was in thirty minutes. With a burst of energy, I quickly dressed and headed out the door. I could not pass up the opportunity to attend. I'd always enjoyed the sermons from this pastor because the messages were different from other faith leaders. His presentation always felt like feel-good storytelling with a message of hope and faith. When I arrived at the sprawling church campus, I didn't know where to park or what building to go into, but somehow, I made it inside.

This was the first time I'd ever set foot in a Christian church. I wore all white because I had a vague sense from my American peers back in high school that one wore white to church on Easter. Other than that, I had no idea what to expect. I didn't know what, if anything, I needed to do, and I didn't know how long the service would last or what would happen. I just took my seat in the back—and trusted. Almost as soon as the sermon began, I started to cry. I didn't even know why I was crying. Tears flowed from somewhere deep inside me, and I couldn't stop them. I cried through the entire service, and then Pastor Joel Osteen asked, "If you would like to give your life to the Lord, stand up."

I didn't even know what that meant. All I heard was "Stand up," so I stood, still crying. The person next to me lovingly said, "Oh, it'll be alright, honey. God has blessed you." When people started to leave the service, I thought it must be like an intermission, where people get up and go to the bathroom or get a glass of water and come back. So I stayed. Within a few minutes, a new crop of people filed into the auditorium and a second service began. Just like the first, I sat through it and cried through the entire message.

When the last service finished and I headed home, I didn't know what was happening to me, but I knew I wanted more. From then on, I attended Lakewood Church weekly and soon joined the choir. I bought a Bible and started reading it and became fascinated by this new faith and my emotional response to it. Still, I had many questions. To answer those questions, God put someone in my path, someone who was generous with her time and willing to help me. That person was a woman named Rhonda, a receptionist at our office who was literally right in front of me when I went into work each morning. Although she hadn't approached me about her religion, she wore a cross and occasionally mentioned a church group. Hesitantly, I asked her my first questions about this faith I found myself so drawn to.

For two years, Rhonda patiently answered all my questions, listened to my doubts and fears, prayed with me, and shared with me the story of her own walk with God. Not once did she tell me, "Hold on," or "Just wait five minutes." Whenever I needed her, she was there, ready to give me advice and counsel. I was fascinated by the figure of Jesus, but I couldn't understand him, at least not yet. His sacrifice intrigued and puzzled me. I didn't understand how someone could give his blood for people he'd never met, and I didn't get how his blood could cover all of humanity. What did it all mean? Rhonda was there to answer the many questions, and she shared her own thoughts with me. She even taught me how to pray.

I can't thank her enough for her generosity and guidance during that time in my life. I'd need every bit of faith I could muster for what would happen next.

Kidnapped!

This next part of my story could come straight from a Bollywood movie, packed with drama, cross-border suspense, unthinkable twists, and of course, a final climactic moment. It was the longest and most difficult phase of my life. The events that took place were heart-wrenching, to say the least, but I share this to show circumstances like this do exist in real life. And just like in the movies, there's always a way out. Happy endings can come true with faith and persistence.

Although my divorce was final, the custody battle was not. During the divorce, I had full custody of Bhakti, and my ex-husband had full custody of Sharayu. Funny how cultural strongholds show up. I was allowed to bring Sharayu with me to Houston for one academic year, as long as I didn't change my married name back to my maiden name. Given I was divorced, that restriction didn't make sense, but my focus was on my girls. Having them both with me, I hoped that by the time the school year was up, I'd be able to keep Sharayu with me in the States, but my ex had other ideas.

In June 2010, he notified me that he was coming to the US to visit his cousin in Austin, Texas, and he wanted to take Sharayu with him for two weeks. I felt no harm could come from it, so I agreed. But when I hadn't heard from them in two days, I felt extremely uneasy and called his cousin. I was horrified to learn there were never any plans for them to visit Austin. I then called his mother and learned the shocking truth. My worst fears were confirmed. Sharayu was already back in India. I had been duped. He'd kidnapped our daughter, saying she was an Indian, despite the fact that she was born in the US.

Once Sharayu and her father reached Indian soil, the US no longer had jurisdiction and my case didn't mean anything in terms of enforcing the custody ruling. I immediately contacted the American Embassy in India and asked for their help, but just like a Facebook relationship status, things were complicated. By that time, my green card was being processed, and I was waiting for an interview. Not yet a legal American citizen, I faced a great deal of complexity with governmental cross-border and international issues, which prevented me from flying out of the country. This is how that one car accident, which changed my birthplace from the US to India in a split second, impacted my life and my children's lives in the most unimaginable ways.

Bhakti was in India for her summer break. So it was decided between my US and India council that Sharayu would travel back to Houston with her sister. They both were to board a plane together to come back to Houston, and Sharayu would continue school in India with her dad after summer break. The flight departed on August 13, at 2:00 a.m., which meant the girls had to leave Pune on August 12. The Indian courts had granted their departure on August 13, not the 12th. Therefore, when Bhakti arrived at her dad's house to pick up her sister on the way to the airport, she was not allowed to do so. Heartbroken, Bhakti left Pune on her own and headed to the Mumbai airport. Sobbing, she called me. She could wait no more, or she would miss her flight and neither of my girls would return to the US. I, the lioness, could do nothing in that moment to protect my cubs. We both were helpless.

Reaching Sharayu to check on her was impossible. Her father had gone overseas for business and had instructed his house staff not to allow me to speak with my daughter. This was the start of a five-month ordeal in which Sharayu was continuously moved between different relatives to keep her hidden from her sister and me. Two sympathetic family members, lionesses in their own right, managed to check on her and get messages to me of her well-being. In return, I sent messages back: "Tell her I'm coming to get her myself." Whenever Sharayu was in their care, I spoke to her briefly. It broke my heart to hear her beg to come home with me. Knowing Sharayu was safe and in good hands with these women comforted me. To this day, I cannot thank them enough.

The American Embassy consul general notified me that they were sending a letter to my ex and a representative to Pune to make sure Sharayu was well taken care of, but they first had to get permission from my ex because they needed to come into his house. He wrote them a letter, instructing them not to interfere in his family matters. With that, the American Embassy had to stand down. I had lost twice—once in Houston when she was taken, and a second time when she was not allowed to fly due to a date technicality that put my daughter in the position of property to be moved around. I was determined not to lose a third time.

In September 2010, I became a US resident, and I left for India immediately. Once I arrived, my ex refused to let me see Sharayu. He did not let her go to school either, thinking I would get a chance to take her from there. He took her passport and held her hostage, keeping her isolated in one room for the next five months. From there, the real negotiations began.

Our house in India was still in my name because I'd paid to have it built from money my family had given me. My ex offered to give me my daughter if I gave up the house and all other marital assets, in addition to all my shares in his company, which I had rightfully earned. To know that he would bargain like this with his own child sickened me. It also ignited within me a roaring threat that the lioness within was prepared to take on. I regularly flew back and forth from Houston to India, working with the legal system to free my daughter. Like a character in a James Bond movie, I covered my tracks, changing locations often because he would send people after me no matter where I stayed in India. It was a crazy time that called for crazy ideas.

Being married is so important to the culture of India that my status as a single mom did not cast a positive light on my custody case. The courts wanted me to have a certificate showing I was married. I was still friends with the man I'd met years before, who had given me a glimpse of hope about what a relationship could be, and on a phone call, while I updated him about everything going on, he said, "Enough of the crap. You've gone through so much. As soon as you get here, we will go to court and get married. That way you can go back to India and show you are a woman of character, married and stable, not someone just out and about trying to figure out your life." We did genuinely care about each other, and it was so considerate of him. So, in January 2011, we got married.

As a newly married woman, I went back to India to face the ongoing battle. In the middle of negotiations was my dream house, my vision and creation, which I intended to be a nest for my children. Its walls were a point of pride and identity. I was emotionally attached to it, and the thought of legally separating from it filled every cell of my body with hurt and pain. My ex-husband was using it to control me. Four years had passed since I last saw my beloved home. By now, it had grown quiet and dull, the garden had wilted, and the studio stood empty and thirsty for life. It was deteriorating, and frankly, through the fight for it, I was afraid of deteriorating with it.

My best friend dropped by one day to check on me and said, "Rani, you don't look like yourself. Let me remind you of how strong you've been. Anyone in your position would have either given up or settled. You may not like what I'm about to say, but I have to ask. Is the house really worth all the stress and hurt? You've anchored your identity to an object that you created, but your creation is merely a reflection of you. It will always be with you as you evolve into your next season."

She was right. Another gift of my mind is, once I comprehend a concept, I swiftly take action. What's the point in waiting once I've learned my life lesson? A few weeks later, I signed the release and let it go.

With each passing day, it became more vital that I get Sharayu out of India. I lived in fear that my ex would take her even farther away, this time to some place I didn't know about, and I would never see her again. She lived an increasingly solitary life in India, all in his delusional effort to keep her hidden and safe, which really meant away from me.

Meanwhile, in America, my father was being pressured by some of my coworkers at WOM who believed my custody battle was interfering with my ability to do my job. Dad called to tell me he'd decided to cut my salary by nearly half. It was a devastating blow. He explained that others felt I was not putting enough time in, and it looked as if I was being given a pass just because I was the boss's daughter.

"This is the right thing to do so we are sending the right message," he said. "You have to be the role model. If we give you an exception, we will have to give everyone else an exception. It all starts with you."

I wanted to say, "You know, there are other people who are not putting in half the time I am but are still getting raises and titles." But I was not in a position to argue, and I didn't think it was worth arguing over, so I accepted and made do with substantially less, all while keeping up my normal workload and traveling as often as needed.

Back in the Pune court, I argued I could provide a better educational experience for Sharayu in Houston. To prove this, I was willing to pay two years of tuition in advance at an excellent private school. Before leaving Houston, I had already worked with the teachers and administrators to create a detailed plan for getting her up to speed academically, assuming she would need to catch up since she hadn't attended formal school while with her father. I was no longer seeking full custody; I had long since realized that was not going to happen. I just wanted her to live with me in peace and safety, without fear.

At the lowest point of my journey, on the evening before the final day of the court hearing for Sharayu's partial custody, I desperately needed a sign of hope. I had a Bible on my side table, and when I flipped it open, my eyes landed on a chapter about God's promise to give me my child and many more children and to enlarge my tent, that I should not be afraid for I would not be shamed, no weapon formed against me would prosper, and my husband is my Maker (Isaiah 54:1— 17). This was my sign. In an instant, I felt confidence and peace, which I had not felt in any of the earlier court hearings. The whole chapter, from verses 1 through 17, would unfold in all the years after that day, but at the time, I had no idea what any of it meant. Today, I can say I've lived it completely.

After five long years of legal battles, on February 14, 2012, Valentine's Day, in exchange for every material possession I had, the courts finally granted me the right to take my beloved daughter home with me. Oddly, her father retained sole custody, but she was granted the right to live with me for her education, as long as I could prove I was a respectable person and was emotionally and financially stable. The lioness had her cub back; the rest we would figure out as it came.

I had overcome threats, family politics, and high-court games of delay in attempts to make me give up. I had seen the power of a chauvinistic society in which an honorable woman judge quickly sided with the man, candidly declaring that women who spoke up for themselves, as I had done, were arrogant and overly smart. I became more resilient, avoiding becoming prey to murky deals laced with manipulation and systemic corruption. On this evening, decree in hand, all the drama came to an end. Custody orders signed and sealed, my daughter and I left for the airport. No one in our family thought we would leave so quickly, but I had been waiting for this moment. We were free to go home, and we were going, now—or so we thought.

When we reached the airport, our tickets and passports were verified at the airline counter as our bags were checked in. With a skip in our step, we walked the corridor toward security. Placing our carry-ons on the scanner, we went through the female-only lane for a metal swipe and then retrieved our belongings and went to the final immigration check.

"State your name. How long were you in India? Is this your child?"

I answered politely, and proudly spoke the monumental words of triumph. "Yes, sir. She is my daughter, and we are headed home."

He looked at me, closed my passport, stacked it with some papers, and said, "Follow me."

In an instant, I felt dread in my stomach. We followed the officer and were advised to sit in a tiny, windowless room. The officer told us we were not allowed to leave the country because both our names had been placed on the no-fly list. This was clearly another deceit conjured up by my ex, his last shot at me, one more roadblock to toss onto my path. Undeterred, I explained my background and the court ruling just hours before. But one small detail blind-sided me.

The officer said, "This child's passport does not match the one on the order."

I was shocked. "What?" I asked to see the paper in his hand. It was her passport number, but not the renewed one that had been presented to court. How did the judge get the old number? It didn't even cross my mind to check the digits. I explained it was an older number. I was carrying the entire case file with me in the event anyone asked, and I had a copy of the old passport, which I showed him. "Here, you can verify it belongs to her."

But the officer didn't listen. Instead, he took us to another room. This time, a female officer came in and asked my daughter to sit to the side. I had experienced far too many times the scorn of women against other women, so I didn't have any hopes of gender sympathy.

Without looking up at me, she asked, "What is the issue?"

While she was engrossed in writing and reviewing some papers in front of her, I poured out my heart and explained the whole story again. Under my breath, I prayed for mercy because all I had was the truth. "Ma'am," I pleaded, "please understand. Maybe you are a mother or can understand a mother's heart. If we don't get on that plane, I don't know when we will be able to go home." It was now 2:00 a.m. and my eyes were tired. Our flight would close in forty-five minutes.

All of a sudden, eleven-year-old Sharayu burst into tears and stood up. My daughter had already been through so much and just wanted to go home with me. The idea that she might get pulled back into a life of isolation was too much. Between sobs, Sharayu insisted she was supposed to go with me and had been waiting for this day for so long. All the fear, uncertainty, anger, and sadness she felt came pouring out of her. She was begging to be heard and acknowledged in the way she hadn't been by anyone during this entire process.

Without a pause in her sentences, Sharayu spoke with passion. "Ma'am, please, you have to understand that we need to go. If you don't let us go, no one will, and we just cannot stay here anymore. We've had patience. We have suffered enough. You have to understand. You have to have a heart. Let us go." Her appeal to leave India came through clear as day. Her eyes asked for help, and she wouldn't stop until the lady officer empathized with her.

As Sharayu spoke, the woman listened, and I could see a change wash over her face. I could have shown the officer a mountain of paperwork, but it wouldn't have conveyed our predicament as eloquently as one anguished little girl.

When Sharayu finished, the woman looked from me to the door. Then, quietly, the sound of the chair scooting across the floor filled the room. The officer handed us our passports. With a resolve in her voice and an uncanny glimmer in her eyes that typically comes from experienced wisdom, she said, "You were not here. Go." She called the airline immediately and instructed, "Hold the plane. I'm sending two passengers. Make sure they board."

We thanked her profusely and ran through all the lines toward the breezeway. Finally, we stepped over the threshold and onto the plane, where we were kindly shown to our seats. Once settled in, we sobbed, clasped each other's hands, and waited.

I've flown many times, and I've often experienced that little quiver of anticipation in my belly when the plane lurches forward and begins to taxi, but I've never felt such a rush of relief as I felt when that flight lifted off the ground. Nearly twenty-four hours later, we landed in Houston, passed through immigration without issue, and walked out of the airport into a beautiful and breezy Houston evening. An hour later, as we entered our home, we heard a resounding "Welcome hoooomme!" All Sharayu's friends were waiting for her, celebrating her with balloons, hugs, happy dances, and overjoyed tears. One mom said to me, "You both moved mountains!" With a deep sigh of contentment, I had never experienced before, I agreed.

Pursuing Higher Education

By this time, it was clear that work and education were my clearest path to full independence and the recovery of my daughters. My custody battle would be a constant struggle, since Sharayu's custody remained with her father until she was eighteen years old.

A woman pursuing a divorce was automatically morally suspect for many Indian courts, and my ex-husband constantly argued that my lifestyle was somehow inappropriate for the girls. I did everything I could to show the courts I was a serious, career-minded person who put her children first. Obtaining a degree would demonstrate my commitment and stability in Houston. Plus, the more time I spent with my father's company, the deeper my interest in the business grew. I genuinely wanted to excel, and in a corporate structure, that meant getting an advanced degree.

Weekdays were simple for me: work and home. I spent weekends pursuing hobbies like painting, singing, dancing, and gardening. Email reviews, cleaning, laundry, and cooking were designated for Sunday as prep for the week. The girls and I caught up during evening dinners. We had much to be grateful for, and things were going smoothly. Work settled into a good routine. While I appreciated the ordinary, I continuously looked for ways to improve myself. An effective way to better myself was to figure out what was missing.

As the HR manager, my day was filled with meeting people. WOM was a little over thirty years old at the time and had a vast spectrum of employees. There were people I knew and grew up with while I worked at WOM through my teenage years, and there were new faces with varying backgrounds and expertise who supported WOM's growth. At the Houston location, WOM had over three hundred employees, eighty percent of whom were tenured over twenty-five years. The rest were newly graduated engineers. One of WOM's strengths was (and continues to be) its diversity. I interacted with people from over fifty countries. The majority spoke English; however, each had a unique identity nuanced by their culture and professional skills. I wanted to understand their jobs, expectations, and areas for improvement and growth.

For the most part, WOM's people were complacent with daily ins and outs. They praised the owner for looking out for them like family.

This sounded nice, but oddly, they came in when they pleased and left at five o'clock sharp. Some people worked in silos with little to no inspiration or motivation to get to know each other or learn from one another. Others prided themselves on providing quick, maverick solutions to problems. Then, there were those who were happy to keep their heads down, doing what was required, but not inspired to go above and beyond or try to resolve issues. They were just getting a monthly paycheck. Things needed to change.

I took on a self-prescribed project to interview all three hundred team members. To do my job better, it was important for me to know what was going well, what needed attention, and the underlying causes. The only way to get real information was to get it directly from the employees and to truly listen and learn from them. WOM was no longer the mom-and-pop shop I grew up in. The company reflected its people, but the waters of WOM were moving much faster than its people could keep up with. Merely getting things done was no longer sustainable. This atmosphere created small cliques of temporary heroes and caused large groups to struggle with long-term viability and work satisfaction. Most were proficient, but some needed additional training.

We needed an upgrade, an enhancement of skills and systems to support WOM's growth. I decided this would have to start with me, but I didn't quite know where to begin. Through the interviews, I hoped to find a mentor within the company. Instead, I realized I would have to seek guidance beyond our walls. I read articles about leadership and business strategies, but it was not enough. There was so much I didn't know, and school seemed the place to discover what I needed. When I was seventeen years old, I'd had a great desire to attend Rice University in Houston. Over the years, I felt like I let myself down by not fulfilling that dream. Having moved to India and gotten married years earlier, I thought I had missed my chance. Now, back in Houston, I was ready to move forward with this goal.

Attending a reputable college was intimidating. The last qualifying exam I'd taken in the United States was the SAT in high school. I received my undergraduate degree in India and graduated in the top ten percent of my class, but my commitment was minimal, to say the least. Now, I couldn't believe I had to take my next major exam, the GMAT, at the age of forty. Despite ten years of successfully running a dance company and an additional five years of management experience in an oil and gas company, I had to prove my math capability. The thought of having to relearn college math after twenty years, even though I had a natural aptitude for numbers, was daunting. Additionally, I had family and work to think about. I wanted to provide a good example to my daughters and didn't want to lose out on the great strides I'd made at work. I wondered if I had the courage to do this.

A large part of me said, *It's too late*. The other part said, *If you want to be your best, Rani, you have to learn from the best*. I had to be my own cheerleader. So I made the decision to give it my all. If I was getting an MBA, it would only be from Rice University because it had one of the top-rated MBA programs in the nation.

On my next birthday, I announced my plan. Almost instantly, people started whispering. "Why does she need an MBA? She's the daughter of the owner. She can do what she wants." Some suggested: "She could sit at home and still be fine. Why is she so bothered about working?" Others questioned: "What is the MBA going to do for her anyway?"

I couldn't quite understand why people wanted to limit my identity. What did my relationship with the owner have to do with my skills and talents? Their comments inferred that I was entitled, as if there was no reason for me to be passionate about growth, knowledge, and making an impact. I knew I couldn't piggyback off my dad's identity and success, and that is what propelled me to pursue my own.

For two months, a tutor helped me with practice tests for the GMAT. Some days, I felt utterly stupid and not equipped. By the time I got through one problem, I'd forgotten the steps to the last one. I practiced in the morning, between breaks at work, and every evening. Finally, my test day came, and I was as ready as I could be. This was the last eligible date to submit test scores with my application. I reached the center early and was one of the first in line. When I showed my ID to the examiner, he said, "You're not a citizen."

I replied, "No, sir, I am a resident."

With a calm face, he said, "We need to see your permanent resident card." My confidence crashed. I didn't have the actual card with me, and I lived forty minutes away. I called a friend to bring it to me since there was no way I would make it through morning traffic in the fourth largest city in the US. Each second of the following hour trickled on for what seemed an eternity. Doubts muddied the clarity of my composure. I started to think maybe the MBA was not meant to be and I should have left my dream in the past.

Finally, my friend arrived with the card. I showed the examiner and went to my testing station. I was thirty minutes late for a three-hour test. My palms were sweating. Despite my mind replaying the stress and anxiety, I inhaled deeply, exhaled slowly, and approached the test with confidence. This was my chance to move to the next level of my life, and I was ready.

In a few weeks, I gave a huge sigh of relief when I learned I'd passed. Victory! Well, almost. To complete the application for Rice, I needed references. I didn't know many people in Houston who would vouch for my professional credentials, as I'd spent the majority of my adult life in India. I narrowed it down to my boss—my father—and my professional advisor, who was like a second father to me and had known me since I was a toddler. I approached them with a shimmer in my eyes, excited to let them know I was applying to Rice University. Both of them were pleasantly surprised and were happy to send the letters.

As soon as word spread of where I was applying, the second round of whispers began. "Rice? Who is she kidding? She is too old. She has two girls to take care of. She is not smart enough or experienced enough. She is about to get a rude awakening." Instead of breaking me down, those cruel words fueled my fire. I have never understood what pleasure people get from judging others for trying to better their lives. Despite it all, I persisted.

One evening, my daughters noticed my doubt and hesitancy and said to me with firm direction, "Ma, you are not what people say you are. Maybe you are not as experienced in the United States, but you are going to school to learn, to discover more of you. You are you. Your education is yours."

Those were wise words out of the mouths of babes. When I asked them where that insight came from, they replied, "All your life, this is what you have told us and everyone around you. We are just reflecting your words back at you." Their words warmed my heart and further inspired me to step out of those negative reflections and into the light that aligned with my identity.

Within weeks, I was notified of my acceptance to Rice. It was gratifying to see my father's pride in me. He was never effusive; that wasn't his style. But I knew he was proud. I could tell from the quietly contented way he told people about my acceptance. "Whatever she sets her mind to do, she does." Considering that, just a few years before, I had shown up on his doorstep, penniless, with an ugly divorce enveloping my life and a questionable reputation, it seemed almost like magic that I'd been able to make my dad proud of me again.

When I began my MBA program, my life was neatly divided between two spheres. If I wasn't at work or school, I was home with the girls. Doggedly focused on my goals, I was absolutely unapologetic about my priorities. To my surprise and delight, the people around me respected that. Others in my program (mostly male) had similar situations and would politely decline social engagements because of a child's soccer game or an unbreakable bedtime routine. I began to see being a mother with a career wasn't impossible. I wasn't asking for the moon; I was trying to do what most professionals with families do. This was not only attainable, but it was also admirable and healthy.

While I was in school and working full time, my identity shifted. I grew intellectually and explored new ideas and interests. Learning opened my mind and revealed parts of me I didn't know existed. This impacted every area of my life. In 2013, my second marriage dissolved amicably, as we both knew its purpose had been served, and we both had very different expectations and desires in life. Once that chapter of my life was complete, I had neither the time nor the interest to pursue any real possibility of another relationship. I held stubbornly steady to my values, and I was not interested in temporary flings.

In 2014, I graduated. I presented a new version of me to people: beaming, proud, and ready to take on whatever was next in life. But behind closed doors, I let my steel walls fall and felt my successes, failures, and efforts wash over me in a tidal wave. I sobbed, breathed, and let out all the anxieties and doubts that had plagued me from the beginning. I had made it—it was all me. Instead of drowning in other people's words and their perceptions of me, the knowledge and insights I'd absorbed had transformed me. I had learned what it was to rise above, and I had risen. I had freely transcended constraints and boundaries by my own right. My healing journey had led me to this. I was my best self, my highest self, and I was equipped for the ride.

Timeless

August 29, 2002
1:30 p.m., Pune, India
(For women over forty years)

Timeless . . . are the eyes,
Sensuous, stunning, wise.

Timeless . . . is the smile,
Whose spirit crossed many miles.

Child, sister, woman, mother,
Friend, partner, mentor, lover.
Then . . . now . . . forever.

Dearest Daughters,

Come, my child. Rest.

You've gone through so much. When you didn't have questions, and you were sure of what had to be done, everyone else questioned you. But you kept going. You didn't settle. You searched for your center and fought as peacefully as you could to maintain your core.

You inspire me, my dear. Even though many may go through tough times, yours is unique to you. No one can compare or even come close to understanding the pain, the guilt, and the shame you put yourself through. Despite the unjustified unforgiveness, you lifted yourself, somehow held onto a resolve that things would be better, and persevered. That is love. Love perseveres, never gives up, never fails.

It's not easy to choose to stay steady in the middle of a fire. You had to patiently and firmly lead within each situation to let time take its own course for the flames to die down. There were no shortcuts. I wish I could have been there for you to show you the light at the end, to uncover how all these harsh experiences are setting you up for your greatest successes that are so close.

Change is hard. So, if you see someone else going through this phase, open your heart and share your story. As you do, you will find more love for yourself. It's like you will hear you speak to you. Then, forgiveness will surface for things you didn't know you needed forgiveness for.

All this, my dear one, brings you closer to freedom and happiness. It's a transformation, a journey toward wholeness. You're not there yet, but gosh, are you on your way. I'm soooo excited for you! At this point, you are more empowered to listen, to reflect love, and to hope because you are!

Going forward, it's about reflection, not depletion. Of course, it takes practice and constant awareness since this is new to you. But keep going, you are in a wonderful phase. In the most natural way, it's all part of your legacy, and it's contagious!

So again, rest a bit. You deserve it, my loved one.

Love always,
Rani

Chapter Seven:

WHEN I BECAME A DAUGHTER
FORTY-TWO TO FORTY-NINE YEARS OLD

For I know the plans that I have for you . . .
to give you a future and a hope.
~ Jeremiah 29:11

Daughter, the female child, was one of my earliest identities. It was the bedrock of my understanding. The desire to be a better daughter was a significant engine driving so many of my choices and efforts over the years. Only over the last few years have I begun to think differently about what it means to be a child, specifically a girl-child, and identified the most important Father in my life.

For most of my life, my relationship with my earthly father felt like Zeno's paradox. Zeno's paradox is a sort of thought experiment often taught in early physics or philosophy classes, and it goes this way. Imagine you want to walk to the corner store and buy a newspaper. Before you can get to the store, you must get halfway to the store, right? And before you can get to the halfway point, you must get halfway to the halfway point, or one quarter of the way to the store. If you keep dividing the distance endlessly, down to the space of an atom, you can never reach the halfway point. Thus, in theory, you can never reach the end point. The longer you try, the more you are rendered effectively motionless, and you still don't have your newspaper. That's what my relationship with my father felt like.

No matter what I did or how hard I worked, even in the flashes of time when my father seemed genuinely proud of me, I felt as if I couldn't make any real progress in my relationship with him. My final destination of being a beloved and cherished daughter to a proud father seemed more hopelessly out of reach with each step I took. It was as though closing the distance was physically impossible and I was just beating my head against that impossibility. Still, I couldn't stop trying.

Giving up on our relationship would mean abandoning not just the goal I'd had for as long as I could remember—proving myself to my father and being and feeling loved by him—but also letting go of what I thought of as a fundamental identity. The struggle to get closer to my father was what being a daughter meant. This was partially a feature of my specific family dynamic, but it was also, in some ways, cultural. The eldest child, especially the eldest daughter, in an Indian family has a unique responsibility to her parents, and that responsibility shapes the relationship. Being a daughter amounted to striving and falling short and striving again. In many ways, the journey and its endlessness were the point.

By the time I reached my early forties, most of my efforts to get my father's elusive approval centered around our shared work. It had always been easier, somehow, to interact with him in the professional world. There, we had a shared vocabulary, a clear set of expectations and objective measures for success or failure. Even when I was younger, we'd always had an easier time talking about school and my professional future than any other aspects of our lives. This only became more pronounced as I grew older and my personal life became more complicated.

I'd been surprised and pleased by the way my father supported me through my divorce and custody battle. However, that situation wasn't something we could exactly bond over. Instead, I focused on making myself indispensable at work in hope that, by proving myself there, I would finally get the recognition from my dad that I'd been chasing my entire life.

By the time my divorce was settled, I was in the home stretch of my MBA and was ready to immerse myself full time into my father's company. There was quite a bit of work to be done. For many years I had observed my father building and expanding his business—spreading first across the United States and then across the globe. He had done amazing work due to his clear vision of what he wanted to build. However, there was a whole administrative and managerial realm of the business that my father rarely saw because his focus was on innovation and growth, a different level of operations. As the company grew exponentially and became more complex, with additional locations and more employees, the administrative and interpersonal challenges grew well beyond what he could handle.

Enter Rani with a newly minted MBA, a passion for working on human dynamics and group cohesion, and an even greater passion for being useful and effective. I didn't try to revamp what existed, which amounted to an ad hoc system with no centralized rules or guidelines. Instead, I poured my energy into creating a new human resources and professional development system for the company. At the same time, I cleaned up and streamlined our financial infrastructure, which also naturally involved doing a lot of personnel housekeeping. It was a massive undertaking. I asked a lot of tough questions and spent a tremendous amount of time untangling how people resolved logistical problems. Often, these short-term solutions left us vulnerable as a corporation and had to be reversed or massively revised.

Doing this type of work in a high-level corporate setting was interesting, especially in the context of my gender. In some ways, it was almost stereotypical; a woman working with people and systems, developing human resources. That was the kind of "soft skill" women are supposed to excel in. At the same time, coming into a fixed order that had calcified into "normal" over years, and then making big and often scary changes to that order, led to a lot of difficult, confrontational interactions with employees. Many times, I found myself dealing with situations precisely because my father didn't want to wade into them and manage the potential conflict himself.

The position I most often found myself in during this time was not unlike the position I had occupied for so long in our family: intermediary and right hand to the primary authority figure. My femininity was uniquely valuable in those roles as well. Despite being part of a male-dominated industry and company, I was determined to maintain the external markers of who I was—a woman. I dressed professionally, wore my hair long, did not mask my face with makeup, and made no effort to neutralize my body or sense of style. More importantly, I took an approach to management that came naturally to me, striving to engage with people without disrespecting them or putting them on the defensive. I prioritized understanding, consensus, and collaboration above domination or subservience. Instead of focusing on winning, I focused on building the team.

My work ethic and philosophies as both team member and coach made me more successful in my efforts. I was very clearly my father's child. Being his child meant that, even more than typical, I was seen as a surrogate for him, and my words were presumed to be approved and endorsed by him. This made people less likely to dismiss me or try to go over my head because my relationship with my father was seen as less ambiguous or vulnerable than if I had just been a trusted employee. This perception wasn't necessarily accurate, but it was useful in discouraging people from impeding the changes I was implementing.

My approach, presentation, and identity gave me an edge in the business, but none of what I was doing was easy or simple. It took a lot of time and a tremendous amount of hard work and dedication to restructure our financial systems and team dynamics across the entire company. The sheer size and scope of what we were doing was daunting. As the sole developer on this project, I had to travel to seven global locations, including the UK, Singapore, and Dubai, to evaluate the situation in each place, introduce our changes, and then guide people through the new policies and structures. The more work I did, the more problems I uncovered.

Prior to completing my MBA, I was already working a standard forty-hour week. Once I finished my degree, my hours ticked up steadily—sixty, eighty, one hundred hours a week—not including the constant travel to our various satellite offices. Each day, I came in early, stayed late, took on big projects, and completed them in record time. I was determined to prove my worth to myself and my family. I wasn't only burning the candle at both ends; I was burning out.

Certainly, no one was forcing me to work those hours or spend that much of my energy on my father's company. I did it, at least in part, because it made me feel good. I also did it in the hopes that, if I worked hard enough and well enough, it would make my father love me in a more demonstrative way. It wasn't enough for me to know in the abstract that my father cared about me and valued me; I still craved his open affirmation and affection as much as I had since childhood. I wanted to know he loved me, not just because fathers love their children, but because I, Rani, was lovable and good and made him proud to be my dad. My mother loved me this way, so I had an understanding of what was possible. Although we had struggled in my teenage years, my mother and I had become genuine friends, best friends even, in my adulthood.

A Desire to Give Back

There comes a time in most people's lives when they recognize what God put them on earth to do. When that fire ignites, it can explode if that desire is held back. I witnessed this with my dear mother. Like me, Mom was always passionate about teaching. She was my mentor and had a gift for making complex problems relatable and interesting. With no formal background, she was self-reliant, street smart, and fueled with creativity.

In spite of her quest to serve others, by the time she was forty-five years old, Mom was empty and felt a deep hollowness. While visiting her for the weekend in India, back when I was still married and my husband was traveling for work, I witnessed a very different person from the mom I had known as a child, a woman whose entire life had come to a crossroads. She had lived her life as daughter, wife, and mother, never giving thought or value to what she wanted for herself—until then.

"I don't have a purpose in my life," she said in frustration. "I'm done living the same life. I cannot find my answers here anymore. I have to seek my purpose, and I need space to find it."

I understood those words at a deep level because I, too, had struggled with finding my own space in the early days of my marriage and as a new mom. I sat on her bed quietly watching, wondering what to say and what might happen next. I had seen her in this state before and knew it was not good.

In a more serious tone, laced with disappointment and frustration, she said, "I have to go, and no one lets me."

At that moment, my mother's helpless cry was evident. She felt drawn to a spiritual path and was seeking answers, but she wasn't giving herself permission to fully live. She was afraid of what my dad would say, what society would say, and who would take care of her youngest child, who was four at the time.

"Mom, go do what your heart says. You've given everyone all you had; it is time for us to give back to you," I said. Without hesitation, my love for her overflowed.

She nodded with determination and gratitude as she put a few things in her small backpack. She grabbed a bottle of water and her flashlight. "I'll be back," she said, and then, she left.

This was in 1994. There were no cell phones, and I did not have a clue where she was going or when she would be back. Would it be hours or days? My siblings were young, but old enough for me to take care of. By that time, Bhakti was a toddler, old enough to play with my younger siblings while I watched them all and allowed my mother the time and space to find herself.

For two days, I piddled around the house, cooking, cleaning, keeping the children engaged, and wondering where Mom was and what she was doing, praying for her safety. When I awoke the morning of the third day and realized she was still gone, I did not panic, nor was I stressed. I experienced God's peace in a new way. That afternoon, Mom walked back through the door, light-footed. A brilliant aura glowed through her skin.

With excitement, she said, "Rani, I found it!"

What a relief! "What did you find?"

She excitedly explained the beautiful discovery of her calling, her purpose, her future. She knew it, and anyone who saw her that day would have seen and heard the brilliance and clarity in her voice and demeanor.

"I will educate poor, underserved children. I will build a school and home for children who have no access to education or who don't have a home," she said.

Ah, she's found her purpose! I smiled in admiration of her giving heart.

When Dad returned to India the next week, we all set out to visit the place where she had been when her divinely inspired idea landed upon her. Early in the morning, she took us to a hilltop a few miles off the main road, away from the city rush, amid the serenity of the mountains. The view was beautiful. There, we discovered the land that would become the site of her school, a twenty-seven-acre space that marked what would become home to many and the beginning of her legacy.

Her school, Vision International Learning Center, was built in 2000 and has thrived since its opening. Over the years, teaching the underserved children in India through her residential school, and educating all ages of the less privileged, has allowed her to realize her life's purpose. She has served dozens of children without access to education, many of whom had no family. Gradually, she housed over one hundred children ranging from ages three to fifteen. Her large heart gave her a large vision, the glow of which radiated and touched others.

Part of the school campus has become a rehabilitation center for adults. Malnourished families from local villages come to work on the grounds. Women and children suffering from domestic abuse find a safe place of respect to heal and grow. Even as her light glows strong within her, she lights sparks of hope within many.

My mother built that school from the ground up, literally. When she purchased the land, it was arid mountain land, beautiful but incapable of growing things. She designed and installed a sustainable drip-irrigation system, which has transformed the property. Today, it is lush and green, and no one would ever guess it was once a dry, thorny vista. She transformed everything else the same way, from the physical buildings to the curriculum. I encouraged and supported her efforts wherever I could, helping her establish financial and legal structures for her foundation as I had done for my father's company. I also mused about a more hands-on way of getting involved.

Years before, after returning to America from India, I was struck by the disparity in resources for children in both countries. It wasn't a universal comparison. Sadly, most Indian children are worse off than the average American child. However, the spectrum of circumstances in India is so much wider and is on display all the time. I saw it when I was a teenager and walked past a slum to my private school, and I saw it as an adult when children of immense privilege took my dance classes along with kids from tiny, impoverished villages. The different economic classes have no choice but to be aware of one another at all times in a way that doesn't necessarily happen in America.

I've long thought there's something inherently valuable in being aware of the experiences of others. How can we effectively understand and work to mitigate poverty if we refuse to look at it? Psychologically, I also understand the value in seeing how people with far fewer resources and opportunities live. Not only can it inspire people with more privilege to use some of those advantages to help others, but it can also make them rethink what might have previously seemed to be insurmountable obstacles in their own lives. If people with far less are thriving in one way or another, despite their circumstances, what excuse do we have for not doing the very best with all we've been given? How much do we really need? What is truly most important in life? Is there a better way to leverage what we have to accomplish our goals?

My heart's desire was to create something of service to people, to help them reach their highest selves. What I didn't want, however, was something unintentionally exploitative or any sort of poverty tourism. I wasn't interested in spearheading a mission trip or a humanitarian effort that had no consideration for what the local people needed and wanted. I was aiming for something more like a classic student exchange. I wanted to launch a program that would benefit American children by exposing them to a centuries-old culture in a vibrant, complicated, emergent nation. I wanted them to meet real Indian people and stay in their homes. I wanted them to connect with Indian children and participate in daily Indian life, and I wanted this partnership to benefit the Indian communities and families in a tangible way.

In 2015, I founded Impact India and started organizing biannual trips to bring interested American students to Mom's school in India for one week. My goal was to identify high school students who might not otherwise have the opportunity to experience this kind of program, kids who were in need of support, direction, or simply a change of scenery. The program started with a handful of students. Over the years, it has grown to the point that my mother had to create a department of international programs through her school. My daughter, Bhakti, now does most of the logistical work for our multiple programs. This collaboration has become an amazing way for three generations of women in our family to come together and build something meaningful.

Even this kind of success couldn't fill the hole in my heart, however. I still yearned for my dad's love and approval. One year, he flew to India to attend the grand finale of one of the international programs. As he looked out at what my mother and I had built, he said quietly to me, "Look at these kids; they are so happy. All of this is going to come back to you tenfold. I know it."

Hearing him say this, I was practically glowing. I had a fleeting thought that this would finally make him see how hard I was working and how much I was doing for him and for my mother. This, I thought, would be the moment he finally told me what a good daughter I was. Instead, nothing changed.

Dad would praise me verbally, and he definitely appreciated my efforts on his behalf with the company, but even after years of hard work, I still didn't have an official job title at WOM. I did have a decent salary, but it was much less than it should have been since it had been cut nearly in half during the custody years. Also, my father didn't want anyone to think he was favoring me simply because I was his child. I wasn't a part of any public-facing materials. I was treated more like a high school kid helping at her parent's restaurant after school than as a qualified, experienced, well-educated adult essentially managing the entire financial, administrative, IT, and human resources apparatus for a multinational corporation.

I tried to reconcile the disconnect between the emotional support and recognition I wanted from my dad and what he was providing. Through all my efforts, I learned some key lessons about leadership.

By 2017, I had been working in my father's company for over ten years and had been recognized as the 2016 Woman of the Year by the Indo-American Chamber of Commerce. I'd started in HR and gradually made my way through every department and visited every WOM global location. It was the best on-the-job training I could offer myself. Not only did I get to know the people, but I also understood the minute intricacies, gaps, and strengths of our business. I made steady changes to increase WOM's growth, and those changes were appreciated within WOM and got attention in society. My passion was to help the company grow, to become more efficient, and to expand with a focus on legacy. I didn't have an official title, but, boy, did I have a vision.

Our salespeople were playing it safe, focusing on the same old clients and legacy customers, but I knew the technology we had developed would benefit larger players as well. Herein lies the struggle within any company, and especially within a family business like ours. How do you assert your position and ideas and implement innovative avenues of progress, especially as a relative newbie and a woman, in a collaborative way?

At this time, the oil and gas industry was struggling to find a balance. There were multiple campaigns to increase diversity at every level, and major producers created special initiatives to include historically underrepresented individuals and entities. I saw this as a huge opportunity for WOM because we had consistently been a widely diverse company. However, no one else on our team saw the value or potential in touting this unique distinction. Typically, something of this nature required internal alignment, with support from HR, marketing, and especially sales. But they all thought our company was too small to stand with the majors on the issue of diversity and was not qualified to go after larger accounts. That didn't stop me.

Through extensive research and after working through mountains of government red tape, my efforts to establish WOM as an underrepresented entity succeeded. My goal was to give us an equal voice and a seat at the table, to have WOM recognized and qualified as a minority-owned, woman-led business. Though the qualifying process was intense, the major drilling producers finally recognized us.

After months of painstaking work, we finally received invitations from two of the largest oil producers, working as a cohort, to drive the diversity initiative forward. Through a number of meetings and interactions over the course of another full year, I developed a relationship with each of these companies and finally gained access to the decision-makers on the executive leadership teams. At this point, word spread within WOM that I was making inroads with sales and landing major contracts. Instead of being excited about the possibilities, the major account managers within our company protested. They complained to my dad, suggesting I was interfering in their sales process or putting their preexisting relationships at risk.

The vice president of sales approached my dad, saying, "Rani is disturbing our process. She is a woman. No one is going to give her the time of day. She thinks she is making good headway, but she doesn't understand the people at the top and will never succeed. We have been in this business since 1980, and she just came in a few years ago. What could she possibly know? We are happy she went back to school and got a degree in finance, but please tell her to focus on that. She should just stay in the office where she belongs." Over the course of the next two weeks, Dad heard this from many folks within the sales department, but he had known what I was doing from the very beginning.

When we became qualified as a minority-owned operation, he celebrated the achievement. It was something he had wanted to accomplish for over thirty-five years. At that point, however, my dad faced a dilemma. He couldn't rock the boat with our existing sales team because they were a solid group. They worked well together and achieved some milestones along the way, but no one was thinking outside of the box. While their focus was incremental growth, mine was expansive. I knew exactly how I would close these accounts and structure these deals. I had been working on it for nearly three years. If I had just one more year, I would cross the finish line with a gold medal on my chest.

Dad called me into his office one day. "Look, Rani," he said. "You have done an excellent job. I'm going to be very direct with you, and this is going to hurt. You are going to have to give up the relationships and accounts you have developed. The sales team needs to take it from here. Trust me, you will come out much better in the long run. There are many other things to focus on. Just focus on the future and keep innovating."

My heart broke again. He didn't understand my struggle. He was asking me to stay in my lane and sit in my office alone. He didn't know what it was like to fight to prove himself, urging people to care enough to include everyone in the conversation, to give us all a chance to share our abilities, our ideas, and our skill sets. I left work that day as quickly as I could and spent the next two days crying profusely. I was angry because all my efforts to prove to everyone in the company that I could help bring balance and diversity to the sector had fallen on deaf ears.

After my pity party, I decided to change my focus. It was time to reassess the situation by asking myself some serious questions. Had I achieved my mission? Yes. I'd wanted to grow the company and open more doors, and I had done that. Was I the only one who could carry the torch? No. The continued growth of the company was not about me. My new mission was to pass the torch, to rekindle the flame within others, and to continue our legacy. That required me to let go—and that hurt.

I then considered how I could move forward with a focus on other endeavors, as my dad had suggested. The time had come for me to explore my next avenue of growth, my next big idea. This seeming defeat could provide an opportunity to establish myself as someone who gives back and opens doors for others. Maybe this was what leadership was about.

These were all good considerations, yet I was left with the dilemma of what to do with the lingering irritation, anger, and resentment I felt. After all, I still had to work with these people who had opposed and undermined me. Without over-thinking it, I decided to put my purpose in front of my pain because pain is purposeful. In that moment, I chose to give up something I had initiated and accept the reality that I am not the creation, but the creator. If I had succeeded in this one effort, and I had, I could succeed again.

On Monday, I returned to the office with a new perspective and attended the sales meeting with my head held high. Instead of frustration, I showed excitement and appreciation for the sales team's commitment to taking the initiative forward. They were initially confused, but eventually came up to thank me. In that meeting, I learned opening doors and giving others an opportunity to shine, passing the ball, and letting others slam dunk was a critical component of my success as a leader, as it continues to be.

The Freeing Gift of Unconditional Love

While all of this was happening, I was still exploring and refining my spirituality. The concept of love and feeling loved was at the center of that exploration. Still very drawn to the teachings of the Bible, I was increasingly interested in the overlap and interplay between Krishna and Jesus, the struggles they faced, the leaders they were, and the values they espoused. I saw them as intertwined, part of the same divine entity that merely adopted different names and faces as needed. I began to understand my engagement in this new faith not as a chance occurrence, but as a part of the continuum that started in my early childhood.

When I began learning about Krishna as a young girl, my parents and religious figures in my life stressed the connection to karma. "What you do comes back on you" was both a warning and a promise, intended to serve as a guide in life. My father used that framing to praise me when he saw me doing good for others, and my parents and other observant Hindus would likewise use this to explain the misfortune or suffering we reap from the sins of a previous life. There was always a reason, always something I'd done wrong, even if I had done it in another life. That way of understanding the world was rooted deep in my mind.

When I was a girl, however, it wasn't Krishna's relationship to karma or reincarnation that fascinated me; it was his capacity for love. Krishna reinforced the importance of putting good in the world to get good back, but he also loved people without consideration for their circumstances. He was a being of play, joy, and music, not one of violence, condemnation, or war. Most importantly, he embraced all of creation without reservation. Not only was he love, but he was also unconditional love, and that was a vital part of Krishna's legacy and teachings. That message largely got lost in the anger of the world and the endless karmic cycle. I believe Jesus existed to break that cycle and to finally bring genuine relief to all humanity.

That knowledge came only after a long struggle for clarity and understanding. From when I was thirty-six years old in 2008, when I first set foot in a church, until I was forty-two years old in 2014, I searched and studied, circling ever closer to a truth that would set me free. Still stuck on the thinking of my childhood—of fault and guilt and inescapable destiny—I couldn't seem to reconcile that with Jesus's ultimate sacrifice. I understood sin. I understood punishment. I understood repentance. But somehow, no matter how hard I tried, I couldn't understand grace. And I still couldn't say Jesus's name.

One Sunday morning, in 2014, as the choir lifted their voices, I sang along. I didn't know all the words, so I created space for my own words. It was fine until the name *Jesus* was spoken. I couldn't say His name. It just wouldn't come out of my mouth. Song after song, I tried to make my tongue, teeth, and breath say, "Jesus," but I failed each time. I was scared. I felt like I was betraying the gods of my Hindu faith, my culture and upbringing. I wanted to push away the feeling of being confined, so I went around my fear and found a plausible solution, replacing Jesus with "He's-us" in the lyrics.

I couldn't understand what was holding me back. There was no apparent reason. No one stopped or restricted me. My upbringing was Hindu, but I was taught to appreciate all faiths. On one hand, I adored Jesus, but on the other, I couldn't bring myself to verbally acknowledge Him. I was frustrated and felt like a hypocrite. The space in my mind felt blocked, as if something else was staring down at me. When I focused on what was occupying that mental space, there they were, all the Hindu gods. I dared not go past them. I was afraid of losing their love and protection.

The moment it finally clicked happened two years later, on Easter Sunday. While reading about Jesus's sacrifice on the cross for the umpteenth time, suddenly, I saw the same words in a different way. When I read Jesus's powerful words, "It is finished," something fell into place inside me. *It is finished*—the message Krishna tried to bring to the world was finally understood, the cycle of sin and punishment I knew so well was finally broken. *It is finished and you are free.*

Now that I had made a breakthrough, I was determined to get around the remaining obstruction. I sat down, Bible open in front of me, and said, "Jesus," over and over. At first, I was just reading it from the book, using the printed words to anchor myself, and reciting the word without really feeling it. I envisioned the Hindu gods standing side by side, next to Jesus, and I could barely whisper the syllables. *Why?* I thought as I struggled to say His name again and again. *Why is this so hard? Please, free me from this struggle.* Then, a voice inside spoke. "Respect your past. Thank it for serving you well. Love all as I have loved you."

"As I have loved you." These words opened my heart as if the heavens had parted and shined upon me. I had never felt such an open, vast space, and in it, I was loved. I was loved! For the first time, I accepted Jesus's abundant, overflowing love. I took in His forgiving and redeeming love for me and understood that I was whole, perfect, wanted, accepted, and loved exactly as I am, now and forever.

Like pedaling hard to work the rust out of a bike's gears, the name slowly started to come easier and easier. As I spoke, I began to cry. This time, my tears were not mysterious to me. As I finally said, "Jesus," the name of the Son of God, I accepted something about myself: I am also a child of God. I am His *beloved daughter*. This knowledge changed everything about my life, but nothing so drastically as my identity as a daughter.

I realized I had been wrong about what it meant to be a daughter. It wasn't about striving and failing, it was about acceptance and peace. I was even wrong about my ultimate Father, my Father in heaven. I had spent my life trying to get things from my earthly father that he wasn't equipped to provide, unconditional love and security in my place as his child, regardless of my struggles or failures. I had expected my dad to be not only a father, but also a Divine Father, when, in the cosmic sense, he was just as much a child as I was.

The liberation I felt with this new knowledge allowed me to forgive myself for flaws and shortcomings I'd so long obsessed over. I now had space in my heart to let go of other hurts I had been holding on to. My father and mother were not God. They were not perfect. They were doing the best they could with what they had at the time, and we were all just striving toward a better way of being. This didn't mean I forgot or excused every negative thing that happened in my life, but rather that I was able to acknowledge it without allowing the pain of it to continue. Jesus had taken all that pain on Himself and what was left was purpose.

Ask and You Shall Receive

With this new mindset, in April 2016, I began to rethink my role in my father's company. Admittedly, I was not happy with the status quo, so I asked myself what would make me happy and what was reasonable for this job to provide. Again, the words of my grandmother came into my mind at the perfect time. *"Rani, tu vishwa kadhun madatichi vat baghates? Pan tu ha vichar kelas ka, ki vishwani tula sagale dila ahe ani tujhi vat pahat ahe?"* "Rani," she had told me, "you're expecting the universe to lend you a helping hand, but have you not thought that the universe has given you everything you need and is waiting on you?"

The answer became clear. I wanted recognition and the security and salary of a role commensurate with my work. I no longer wanted these things in the hopes that they would make me feel loved as a good daughter; I wanted them because I had earned them fairly. If I didn't get what I wanted at my father's company, I could get it elsewhere. I had seen the tug-of-war between my dad, my brother, and the current leadership for years, and I didn't want to add more stress to the situation. So I surrendered my ego into my space of purpose and had faith in a higher hand. In fact, I shared my decision with my father to give him peace of mind in handing the company to the only son of the family, Mahesh, my brother, who was the director of business development for WOM.

I had nothing to lose and every opportunity to find a new place for myself somewhere else. If my father denied my request to let me go, out of my familial and cultural duty and my respect for him, I was prepared to work even harder to set the stage for my brother to take over. Then, I could graciously and respectfully exit onto my next path.

Having a conversation with my father about my role was one of the more difficult things I had ever done related to my work at the company. It was one of the few times in my life I had directly challenged him, and in many ways, it went against my instincts. In other ways, however, it was surprisingly natural. I no longer needed him to give me anything. Instead, I was simply allowing him to correct an oversight.

"Well, what sort of title do you want?" he asked, slightly bewildered, when I addressed the topic.

My father seemed surprised by my request for an executive title and the compensation to go with it. From his response, it was evident that it would never have occurred to him that I deserved more than what he'd already given me.

"What title do you think I deserve?" I countered, curious to know how he saw my role and the value I brought to the company. All this time, I had convinced myself he was holding something back, waiting for me to finally be good enough to earn it. In reality, he wasn't even thinking in those terms.

"Finance manager?" he offered.

That title was for someone who did payroll and kept the books for one office, nowhere near the level of work I'd been putting in.

"Really, Dad? I've financially restructured your company, built new growth strategies, streamlined and standardized internal processes, and regularized admin and human resources," I pointed out.

"Well, what do you think is appropriate?" he asked, clearly stumped to come up with an appropriate title for me.

"Chief financial officer is more fitting for what I do with the company," I said. I let him ponder this for a moment before I spoke again. "The financial heads globally also get direction and guidance from me, so I believe my role should be global."

Dad liked the idea, but his innate concern for what others would think led him to ask, "What about Bob? What will he think?"

Luckily, I had performed due diligence before approaching my father and had respectfully spoken with all the stakeholders who would be impacted by the change. Each had given me their support and agreed to report to me. When I shared this feedback with my father, he agreed that, going forward, my title would be Global CFO of WOM. Almost immediately, my relationship with my father changed, more so due to my mindset than his. My identity was not only as *his* daughter, but as the daughter of *my heavenly father*. This knowledge was empowering, as it was not tied to external validation, compliments, a title, or salary. For the first time, I acknowledge my worth as determined only by me and my faith.

This sense of peace and my newfound ability to advocate for myself encouraged my father to give me more consideration at work. He realized I had the education and skills to go elsewhere and that I was willing to challenge him. Therefore, he began to treat me the way he would treat any other valued employee. Finally, I received the private and public acknowledgment I'd spent my life chasing. Oddly enough, it didn't seem as important to me anymore. I had found affirmation in God and in myself, and that was all I really needed. For the first time in my life, my choices were completely my own.

As Global CFO, I started making changes by introducing systems and processes to ensure more accountability. Unsurprisingly, changes were met with resistance because the business had settled into a status quo developed over years of doing what seemed right and easy, but in reality had become ineffective. Now, I had the title and the support to move forward with my vision to innovate in a way that was respectful of WOM's history and forward-thinking to prepare for its future.

In 2016, WOM was expanding and needed more space to diversify our operations. Our team identified land in India that stretched over hundreds of barren fields, perfect for an industry setup. Dad was spending most of his time in India, where plans were conceptualized, permissions processed, and timelines developed. For WOM, the expansion was a first of its kind. Everything was new, so experienced personnel were scarce. Advisors, consultants, project leads, and support staff weighed options and made decisions in haste. The race was on to complete the massive expansion project before our deadline. The company was on the verge of making the final transaction when the Indian government announced a major strategic policy change. All plans were stopped in their tracks, and our teams rushed to redirect and align to the new policy.

In December of that same year, my father got caught up in the turmoil of India's currency demonetization. One week into the changed winds of regulation, I read the most alarming news in WOM's history. The company's name and its project were splattered all over the news media with false allegations of fraud and money laundering. Accusations were not directed at the key project leads or consultants but at the owner, my father. Clearly, there was a fire, but I didn't know the extent of it. My gut asked only one question: *If everything was working so well, what went wrong? How did things get out of hand?*

I was in Houston when I read the news, and the India legal team soon started texting to advise family members to stay away from India until the team got a grip on the situation. My father, as the head of an international company with roots in both India and America, was in a vulnerable position. So vulnerable, in fact, that almost everyone else associated with the company and the family fled India, leaving only my father behind. He was determined to sort everything out, but I knew he couldn't do it alone.

After all I'd been through, the element of danger did not faze me. I simply gathered the resolve I needed to face it head on. I was positive, yet quiet and resolute when I booked my flight to India. At the time, Bhakti was staying at her college dorm in a different state, while

Sharayu was in high school living with me. I called Sharayu from work, instructing her to pack my bag. Then, I called Bhakti to let her know of my plan. I raced home, gave Sharayu a kiss, and with my girls' blessings, I left for the airport, grateful for my staff, who has always been an intricate part of my support system. They have always had my back and taken utmost care of Sharayu whenever I traveled.

The next day, early morning in Pune, when Dad woke up and walked to the breakfast table, there I was, seated, waiting for him. He was calm but surprised, "You're here? Everyone else left."

I looked into his blue-gray eyes with a smile. "I could never leave you alone, Baba. Whatever it is, we will go through it together."

The following days uncovered the truth of the situation. Several multinational companies had been targeted by the government, including ours. Things were chaotic, and the stakes were high. Over the years, WOM staff had developed a casual approach to operating the business. There was an aggressive focus on production coupled with careless oversight of processes and procedures. Waste, misguided information, and decisions made in the pursuit of power had lasting repercussions. Years of casual, complacent behavior had turned the spark into a wildfire and left my father in the middle of it.

My father was a smart man and a skilled engineer, but when it came to legalities, he took a casual, hands-off approach. Years of that kind of management made way for a huge amount of confusion all around. Although the allegations were false, several mistakes were uncovered. Now, we had to fix them. A big part of my job since joining the company had been sorting out these ad hoc solutions and redoing things properly. Unfortunately, I hadn't worked quite fast enough, and demonetization had exposed some of the biggest gaps and cracks in our systems. I was not directly in the flames but felt the singe of heat. My vantage point on the outside allowed me to work behind the scenes to resolve matters.

Dad had one thing on his side, the truth. We hadn't done anything illegal. We were using our own funds to buy land. My job was to protect our proof and present it to the right people. The biggest challenge was knowing whom to trust. Whenever I requested details or advice from officials, they gave me partial information based on generic speculation or the sheer convenience of taking the easy way out. I could not seem to get a direct answer, which wasn't helping the situation. I quickly realized I would need to search for advisors who understood, cared, and had investigated all angles to help us find the best way through.

I got to work immediately, handling grievances and negotiations on a case-by-case basis, one after another, with barely a pause in between. In all the years I had worked with my father, this was the first time I'd literally worked *with* him since joining the company, and he saw firsthand how I tackled big problems. Through this observation, he came to admire and appreciate my tenacity as well as my work ethic. There we were, the two of us, against seemingly insurmountable obstacles. It was one of the few times in my life when I felt like my father and I were fully on the same team.

Vital to that sense of solidarity, however, was a critical conversation with my father shortly after I arrived in India in early December. By the end of the month, it became clear that our work was going to take some time. I decided to fly back to Houston to spend Christmas with my daughters and return to India in the new year to finish what I'd started. When I told my father this, he reacted in a very familiar way.

"You can't leave now when you've just arrived. And you certainly cannot be gone for five days."

He had a point. We were in crisis mode, and I had a duty to the company. If this had happened a year or two before, I probably would have canceled my flight and remained in India to prove my loyalty to him. But now, I knew what it really meant to be a daughter. It wasn't about guilt or duty, but about peace and purpose. And I knew my purpose clearly.

"I'm going to spend Christmas with my daughters," I said. "I will be back on January second."

Without any further debate, my father accepted my decision, likely because he saw the confidence with which I had begun to make decisions for myself without his approval or support. I was living for me, sharing, and giving because I chose to, not because I had to. That practice changed the way my father looked at me.

It took ten more months to sort everything out in India. During that time, my father and I had the kind of frank, honest conversations I'd longed for but never knew how to initiate. I spoke to him freely about God and my spiritual journey. I think he began to understand that God was my true provider, and I was no longer expecting him to heal me or make me feel good about myself. That, I believe, was a tremendous relief to him because he'd always treated me differently than my siblings and simply didn't know how to course correct or pave a new path with me. I realized then that he had always loved me as best he knew how, and he truly wanted me to be happy. His inability to provide what I needed had hurt him too. Now, as adults, we were together, two children of God trying to get by here on Earth.

For weeks on end, we experienced sleepless nights. Each day challenged us to be patient, to gather more information, and to balance our internal fire. We could not give up. After watching Dad maneuver between authorities, rumors in the papers, and the uncertainty of what was next, the day came for his truth to shine. Finally, after a year enduring the heart-wrenching snail-pace of bureaucracy, the truth prevailed, and in November 2017 all allegations were dropped.

I made a promise to myself that this would never happen again, not to Dad, not to me, not to WOM. Dad had started a company with a commitment to serve in excellence. He had a guiding principle to create a legacy, and I decided that day to carry the torch, allowing it to illuminate a clear path to streamlined procedures and transparent checks and balances.

On Thanksgiving Day 2017, I boarded the plane leaving India to return home to Houston. I fell asleep before I could adjust the pillow on my seat. When I woke up, I asked the flight attendant how much longer we had to land. She looked at me and said, "Oh, you're awake. We kept an eye on you since you barely moved. We land in thirty minutes." I had slept the entirety of the sixteen-hour flight. If there was a word to define that kind of mental and physical exhaustion, mixed with a calm yet exuberant relief, I'm sure it met me in my sleep.

My Face, My Body

Due to the stresses of the India episode, my self-care had taken a back seat. As I looked in the mirror, I did not like what was staring back at me. Always my worst critic, I decided I needed to work out harder and eat less so my clothes could fit better, and so that I could look prettier. When it came to my physical appearance, however, I dismissed the notion of true self-love and looked for acknowledgment from others. *How could anyone be attracted to me? All I do is work.* Like a stone thrown in calm waters, the demoralizing ripple that began in childhood swelled over me once again. My mind flashed back to high school when I was bullied for my looks and foolishly believed I was ugly.

Since there was nothing I could change about my facial features, I focused on the one thing I could change, my body. At forty-five years old, I decided this was the year to get it all back in gear. I signed up for multiple gym classes and decided to really pour it on. Carving time to work out meant earlier mornings and weekend training. Bhakti joined me.

Following one sweat-inducing, high-intensity class, we high-fived after two sets of fifty burpees and ramped our energy back up for the next class, Zumba. For anything to do with dance, I was in my happy place, flowing, prancing like rain droplets over the ocean. My heart pumped blood to a rhythmic beat as I followed the instructor's steps.

Next, was a lunge with hands touching the ground, then lifting high. *Cool dance move*, I thought. *Okay, Rani, you've got more energy to give. Time to take it to the next level.* Heart racing, I touched the floor with pep. As I reached up, I heard a pop.

Instantly, I felt a cold sting shoot down both my legs. My back went numb, and my hips froze. I was in shock. My daughter looked at me, and I motioned with the only thing I could move, my eyes. "I should be okay," I said, hoping to reassure myself. I tried taking a few steps, but I couldn't. I usually pushed through discomfort, but this was unbearable. Bhakti didn't take her eyes off me. I finally said, "Something's wrong." My whole lower body was tense and stiff.

I dragged one leg after the other across the floor, through the door, and down the steps to the locker room. I could feel the rapid onset of inflammation, and my brain went into fix-it mode. From prior foot and knee sprains, I remembered the healing benefit of hot-cold therapy. In the shower, I allowed the cold water to run over my back. Then, I switched to hot water, and repeated this three times. The pain was so intense it felt as if I had pushed a baby out of my back. This express treatment helped for a short time, allowing enough movement to get dressed, walk to my car, and drive home, in spite of excruciating pain. Bhakti followed closely behind in her car.

A few hours later, at the hospital, I was diagnosed with a herniated disk. The doctor prescribed six weeks of bed rest followed by six weeks of physical therapy. For the next eighteen months, which seemed like an eternity, I was prohibited from any and all strenuous activity if I wanted to heal completely. I was so disappointed in myself for allowing this to happen. *This is my body, the one thing I could control!* The entire situation was frustrating, but I knew better than to ignore the doctor's advice and was ready to do, or in this case, not do, anything to fully recover.

In my third week of rest, I passed the time by sleeping off the pain or visiting my acupuncturist to help the healing process. At home, while

I lay on my belly, I had plenty of time to think and meditate. As I prayed for peace over my body, thoughts of work, canceled plans, and intense pain floated through my mind, interrupting the moments of relaxation, and sending me back into feelings of disappointment and rejection. I was a person of action. Why did this happen to me? It felt as if my body was falling apart. I didn't understand what I had done to make it weak. *Now I'll be fat.* Oh, that word. I didn't enjoy mocking myself, but those scornful thoughts came so easily during that time.

Anticipating my first day of physical therapy, I was excited because I knew it would put my body into motion again. When I arrived, walking was difficult, so I had to sit to start the exercises. As if trying to thaw a frozen pipe, every movement was slow, one small maneuver at a time. My legs struggled to move freely as I used my hands and neck to support each shift. Instead of fighting the changes, my body was sympathetic, adjusting to help itself.

In my struggle to perfect my body, I had not taken time to appreciate all it does. Silently, it obeyed every command given. If my mind thought *sit*, it would. If I thought *push harder*, it would. But on the flip side, when my body told me it was tired or ready to stop, my mind didn't always listen. My body took on stress and modified each muscle and cell to support the rest of me. Now, I was forced to notice the changes in my body that I had so easily ignored over the years. I had neglected to give my body the kindness it deserved.

Similarly, I noticed changes in my face. Over the years, my skin had changed, some of my hair had fallen out and grown back, and wrinkles, freckles, and all sorts of marks and crevices had shown up. It was as if I was an entirely different being, unrecognizable as the girl I once was, the young lady, the nimble dancer, the new mother. I realized I had expected my body to stay frozen in the past while my life bounded forward. I was not eleven or eighteen or thirty anymore. I didn't perform and rehearse eight hours a day. This body birthed two babies and went through distinctly unique changes each time. I boasted of being a mother, but I wanted my body to stay that of a teenager. I took on more stress from work's challenges, but demanded my body be as footloose and fancy-free as a child without a care in the world. I had to learn to be patient with my body in order for it to support me.

A few months later, toward the end of physical therapy, I meditated more. As I prayed to trust my body, I began appreciating the changes it had undergone. To properly heal, I had to love my body and see its beauty just the way it was, through my own eyes. I had never taken the time to see myself for myself.

Getting dressed for work was a rote routine to ensure my make-up and hair were in place. But really seeing myself was difficult. Whenever I stood in the mirror, I closed my eyes or looked away to avoid the frozen daggers thrown by the bullies of my past. As an adult, I was still tormented by their childish slurs. Although my back injury had almost healed, my self-image had not. In retrospect, the back injury was an opportunity to stop demanding, to cease controlling, and to step into the mirror of my true self-awareness.

One Sunday, about nine months after the disk injury, I decided to stand naked in front of the mirror, something I hadn't done in many years. I had to summon every bit of my courage to do this because the stronghold of shame held such a hold on my self-identity. Facing myself, seeing my eyes, my face, and my body without any filter, head-on, was one the hardest things I had done in a long time.

With my eyes closed, I approached a tall mirror and spoke the words aloud, "Rani, open your eyes." But I couldn't. After twenty minutes of repeating this command, fear-filled tears dripped down my cheeks, my neck, and onto my bare chest. I finally gathered all I had to open my eyes and face my reflection.

Within a moment, I realized the truth. "Oh," I whispered. "I *am* beautiful." My shoulders dropped and a girlish smile crossed my face.

The feeling of self-nurturing was like that of a mother speaking to her precious child, honest, supportive, loving. The nurturing part of me freed the stagnant waters of self-doubt and flushed the wounds from my past.

"Rani was not born a male" went away.

"Rani is ugly" went away.

"Rani should not have given the security guard flowers" went away.

"Rani should stick to finance, where she belongs" went away.

I saw myself, completely, as the person my grandmother always saw: a beautiful force. My body was beautiful. I was beautiful. Every mark, wrinkle, and previously perceived imperfection made me more beautiful. Each inch of flesh told a story about who I was and who I had become. I was ready to celebrate it all. Unaware of the lifelong damage to my psyche, I, like many women, had allowed myself to crumble and conform under the pressure of maintaining certain looks deemed desirable by society's standards, instead of focusing on my inner self. I had given others power and control over my self-image, but I was ready to take it back.

After about a year of practicing self-awareness, I could freely love myself and adore the changes in me. My body was finally in flow, healed, and healthy, not because I demanded anything from it, but because it was my sacred temple. I promised to remain balanced, to patiently push it to achieve reasonable goals while becoming stronger. No longer would I negotiate being attentive to my body. This was a necessity I practiced daily.

Now, each day I show up for myself, and then I let my body do the talking. Some days, it asks for a three-mile run, a walk, a stroll, or a three-minute yoga pose. Other days, I may need a gentle nudge to get going, but I'm respectful and don't force it. (Although, I do have occasion to show off to my daughters when we fool around doing handstands, headstands, and dolphin arm balances.) The term "fat" is a banned F-word in our home, and the scale is our friend. Changes in numbers are normal and tell me my body is alive and fluid, as it should be. I also confess to having a secret goal to do cartwheels and round-offs till I cross eighty years. But it's a dream, not a demand.

Finding Light in the Darkness

In the fall of 2018, I took a five-week, soul-searching vacation in Bordeaux, France, in a small hillside village in the south, across the majestic snow-capped French Alps. The small town of three hundred people tucked at the foothills of Mont du Chat filled my days with self-reflection and peace.

My room overlooked the turquoise, still, shimmering waters of Lac du Bourget and a wide score of mountains that formed a majestic backdrop against Aix-le-Bains. I soaked in every shape of the clouds through which light beams burst and played. The raindrops danced against the illuminated water, which poured joy into every cell of my being. I took in the colors of the rainbow as its glow hit the earth, unveiling a pot of gold, while a wild gush of wind and rain splatter created more ripples on the surface of the lake in the distance. *"It all co-exists, as do we"* was my gratitude prayer.

At the end of my stay, I was happy, full of light, and ready to return home to Houston. Just before I left France, Pierre-Marie, a family friend and exquisite photographer, gifted me his collection of waterfalls shot in rapid-time still-motion. The photos, printed in rich black and white, intensified the light. Three days after returning home, I sat in my office admiring my new artwork. As I basked in the newness of my mind and my refreshed perception of the future, I was not prepared for the next few moments, which would cast a shadow of darkness upon life as I knew it.

I received a text message from a friend asking if I knew where Mahesh, my brother, was. A few days before, he had left for vacation in Italy to celebrate his thirty-eighth birthday, and messages on our family chat revealed he had landed safely. In response to the text about his whereabouts, I called him but got no answer, and I assumed he was busy celebrating. He would call me back later. Then, I got a call from another of his friends asking the same question and expressing worry. That was odd. So for the next hour, I continued to call and text my brother. No answer.

Finally, I searched his company credit card. As I skimmed the last transactions, I saw a charge in Switzerland. *Hmm, he's probably just out and about exploring and will call me when he has a chance.* I resumed reviewing the day's schedule with my assistant.

An hour later, I heard a knock at the door and, without my response, the head of HR cautiously peered in. Wide-eyed, he said, "There's an officer waiting for you in the conference room."

Curious, I followed him into the room where a stern-faced female police officer was seated. My heart beating in anticipation, I blurted, "Is this about my brother?"

The officer looked confused. "You mean you know?"

"Know what?" I asked. "Is he in some sort of trouble? Just tell me where he is, and I'll go get him." Whatever the problem was, I just wanted to resolve it and get back to work.

"Ma'am, please have a seat," she said.

Why so serious? I wondered. "Sure. Where is he?" I glanced at my watch. In the middle of several important projects, I had things I still needed to do, and this was cutting into my workday.

"Ma'am, are you Revati Puranik?"

"Yes."

"You are listed as next of kin. Are you a kin of Mahesh Puranik?"

My brain whizzed as I frowned. *Am I his kin? I'm his eldest sister, his could-be mother, his friend, his protector. What's kin?* Calmly, I uttered, "Yes, I am." A tinge of seriousness suddenly developed in my throat.

"We went to your father's house, but no one was there. We've been looking for you and found this company address."

I was becoming impatient. *Okay, lady, get on with it. Why is this taking so long?* Yet, my voice spoke clearly. "Where is he?"

The officer cleared her throat, stiffened her spine, glanced deeply into my eyes, and said, "Ma'am, we have received information from the Swiss embassy and confirmed the identity of Mahesh Puranik."

"Uh, okay, that's good. So, is he in jail or something? I can go get him."

"Ma'am, your brother passed away in a hotel," she said.

"Okay, passed what? I can take care of it. Just tell me where he is, and I'll go get him." I clearly wasn't getting it. But the other people in the office with me did.

"Ma'am, your brother is no more. He died," she said again.

In utter denial, I said, "Look, I'm sure he's around. He always is."

And still, she stuck to her story. "He died in Switzerland."

In the fastest second ever, my optimism, my hope, my light went out. I finally comprehended her words, and I couldn't breathe. "What?" I looked at the head of HR.

He nodded. "I'm sorry, Rani. I'm so sorry."

Why does my heart suddenly feel this way? It's going to explode! I couldn't move. I still couldn't breathe. My brain tried so hard to fill my lungs with air, but it seemed impossible in the moment. I was cold, my lips shivered, and my hands trembled. *Why is it so cold? Someone, please turn on the heat, it's so cold in here.* My breath was like a super-slow tidal wave, swelling, then peaking to drop straight down and crash. My inhales were short. The exhales seemed elusive. I was hyperventilating.

"Ma'am, are you okay? Should I call an ambulance?" asked the concerned officer.

For me? My brother's the one who needs the ambulance. Where is he? Trying to regain composure, I managed instead to whisper, "I'm okay."

With a step toward me, the officer handed me a slip of paper. "Here's the number to call and the case number."

I stared at her blankly, like she'd just spoken a language I didn't understand.

"You'll need to call the Swiss authorities to find out more and decide what to do. His body is being held in their facility."

I blinked, confused, numb.

"Ma'am, that's all I know," she said, and she glanced at me with apologetic eyes before solemnly bowing her head and turning to walk out.

It was dark, so very dark that I couldn't see. Everything stopped. Then suddenly, like a flash of light, I thought of my parents. *How am I supposed to tell them?* My mother was staying with my sister, Shubhangi, in Houston, and my father was back in India. I wanted to wait and tell them together, but how could I get my father to fly home immediately without telling him why? My mother was in the early stages of Parkinson's disease, and I wanted her and my father to have the support of the whole family for news like this. I knew I had to tell Shubhangi first.

Time passed in an unknown chasm for me that day. I drove to Shubhangi's home to break the news to her first. We huddled quietly at her home, in a space where our mother couldn't hear the conversation. With Mahesh's body in Switzerland, we had some time to figure out the logistics of our next steps. I called my dad that same evening from my sister's house and made up a story to get him home. I couldn't tell him the truth and have him suffer that pain on such a long flight from India to Houston. He had already had two heart issues and an angioplasty. How could I tell him the son he'd waited so long for, and the prince we all loved so much, was gone? I lied and told him we had a tax issue and the IRS wanted to meet with him. I thought it would be believable because we'd recently been through the demonetization issue.

But he read between the lines. "Put your mom on the line," he said. I want to make sure she is okay."

I handed her the phone, and she said, "I'm ordering pizza!" She had no idea.

Still, my dad agreed to come, knowing something was wrong. The next morning, on his way to the international airport, he called me. "You need to tell me the truth. I can take it. What I won't be able to take is the anxiety, not knowing the truth."

I quickly got my sister on the line, and I got my dad's best friend, our legal counsel, on the line. Then I said, "Dad, this is about Mahesh."

"What did he do, go off and get married?"

Oh, if only, I thought, clenching my eyes tightly.

I said, "He was in Switzerland, and he passed away in his sleep from cardiac arrest."

After a painful pause, my father said, "At least now I know what the truth is, and I am coming. Have you told your mom?"

"No," I replied.

"Wait for me."

Getting my brother's body back from Switzerland was a challenge. No one in my family had any idea how such cases were processed or what was needed to get everything organized in a timely manner. It was frustrating reaching out to the Swiss officials. I worked with various representatives who did not speak English, were in the office less than three hours a day, or had limited experience with this type of situation.

The only thing that made sense was to put my brother's needs and wishes in front of everything else and do what he would have wanted. My love for him became my light. It was the only force that enabled me to take the next steps. I wanted to fulfill his wishes and express my love for him, but maintaining the energy to make the right decisions was arduous.

Mahesh's closest friend, who was waiting for him in Italy, helped me greatly. Though her spirit was shattered, she flew to Switzerland to help claim his luggage. She waited there for days until all clearances checked out, and then she boarded a charter plane with his casket, flying straight to Houston. As a family, we waited at the airport for two hours.

Typically, awaiting the arrival of a family member creates a sense of excitement. This occasion was just the opposite. There would be no hugs, no kisses on the cheek, no questions about the flight or how much fun he'd had in Italy. Only sadness.

After the plane taxied, we watched Mahesh's casket being unloaded from the back of the plane. I've always been aware that each individual comes with a unique destiny, meaning even children from the same parents have their own lives to lead and purposes to fulfill. I tried to take some comfort in the knowledge that I could not live a life for anyone else, no matter how close. We all must walk our own path. However, I never expected his path would be so short.

After Mahesh's funeral in Houston, my parents wanted his final resting place to be in the sacred rivers of India. Our family of twelve, plus one beautifully decorated urn containing his ashes, flew to Pune. Days were heavy but seemed to pass in the motion of getting things done. As traditional responsibilities wound down and people returned to their lives, reality hit me. The real test of emotional strength came after the wake, when everyone went back to their everyday routines.

It is hard to find light during death. When a person's life force is gone, it can draw out all the light around it. In the weeks following Mahesh's death, I clearly saw the darkness approaching, greater than ever. It sat in silence. It waited in the meals my brother loved. It lurked in the songs he sang, and it deepened the grief my parents shared.

My parents suffered pain and guilt over thoughts that they should have done better by Mahesh, and it broke my heart to see their torment. I prayed to never understand the depth of a parent's loss of a child. I stayed in Pune to be with my mom and dad, to help bring some light to their sorrow. I had great faith, knowing a way would be made for them.

As I watched the sunset from my father's balcony, I recalled my life just two months before and the profound light-filled photography I was gifted that hung in my office in Houston. The time-lapsed, black-

and-white image of a waterfall was a spectacle of evidence that light and life are eternal. The choice to see either light peering out of the darkness, or darkness overtaking the light was mine to make. Again and again, I chose to see the light breaking through the darkness. I found peace in knowing that when I seek the light, I will find it, and even death cannot take it away. It is always during the darkest times that I most appreciate the light.

Time came to a standstill when I lost my only brother. I was reluctant to feel or to express myself and my deep grief, so I built a firewall to keep all emotions at bay. People in the company were solemn to my face, but behind my back, the murmurs were loud. "What will happen to the company? He was the only son. Must be devastating to the family, to the father, the mother."

In the following months, I focused heavily on work, my actions powered by my love for Mahesh. That love showed me what to do next. In thirty-eight years, WOM had grown to ten prime locations with three thousand people around the world. Like many fast-growth companies, WOM's weak link was global direction and communication. Work styles varied and sites functioned as independent silos. However, one commonality was the asking of a typical legacy question: Who would run the company after the founder? Following the family tragedy, that question was replaced by assumptions about the founder's ability to run the company.

Somehow, the family grief became an opportunity for individuals to go in separate directions and focus on their own agendas. We had to bring our people together. If the company was to last beyond the founder, we had to correct years of business leniencies. Everyone had to speak the same company language and march to one beat in one direction.

My vision for the company went beyond one generation. I foresaw that the lifespan of WOM could supersede the limitations of the found-

er's lifespan. The company itself could be timeless and cross generations. If I could properly share this vision in a way that would permeate
the hearts of each team, they would become aware of the critical role
they play in the future of WOM. The goal was to protect what my father
had built, to construct a foundation for what would come next, and then
to grow. I wanted to connect more than people; my intent was to connect
generations. However, given the spread of locations around the world
and the number of people within our company, this was my next challenge, my next priority, and I had to figure out a way that would be new
and effective.

Time was precious. People throughout the company made assumptions as to which direction the company would take after such a family
tragedy. I needed to bring stability, trust, and assurance back to the
WOM group and do it quickly. I needed to synchronize my efforts to
ensure a consistent message was received by everyone at the same time.
I drew upon my memory of hoisting buckets of water to fill an empty
tank all those years ago in India. How could I shortcut this critical project for our company the same way I had saved those girls precious steps,
time, and resources? I decided to one-step this by conducting a global
summit. The objective was to get everyone under one roof, uniting
sales, operations, and engineering leads from each location. It would be
a three-day conference focused on issues and solutions forward. This
was the first meeting of its kind for WOM.

Three months after my brother's passing, I announced the event,
which was met with skepticism. Some judged me as insensitive, stating that I was giving more thought to the company than to my family.
The attendance list became more a topic of concern than the conference
schedule and objectives. Given the vibes of hesitation and ridicule, I
wasn't sure how the event would go.

When the event was organized down to the smallest details, the day
came, and I was ready. I communicated to everyone that punctuality and

respect for time were imperative so we could make the most of each session. Presentations offered new information about critical issues within the company. We needed this kind of transparency to move us forward into a new strategy. Each hour was accounted for with a contingency plan outlining redirection if required. People engaged, participated, and were impressed with the flow of the first day, looking forward to the next.

Over the course of the event, one of our greatest areas of opportunity, establishing regular communication around the globe, was successfully resolved. During this three-day intensive event, everyone was accountable. Follow-up was sacrosanct to the success of each goal. What everyone established over three days could not fall back into the gaps. Each participant agreed the summit had been a success and committed to furthering strong communication and collaborative efforts to bring our vision to fruition. As a result, similar summits took place every six months, bridging uncertainties, resolving issues, and moving the WOM enterprise to sustained growth. But my job didn't end there. At the conclusion of that trip, I began to plan WOM's two-hundred-year legacy.

Forged in Fire

For as long as I could remember, I had always been afraid of fire. As a child, I imagined it waiting outside my door or under my bed. I held my breath each time I switched on a gas stove, fearing the flame would spark and cause an explosion. Imaginary fire drills played over in my mind. I could stop, drop, and roll any hour of the day or night.

When I visited WOM's factory, my gut wanted to stay clear of the forge shop, where large chunks of freshly pounded hot metal lined up on either end of the walkway. My whole body shrunk away from the radiating heat. I was terrified of being burned.

I understood all parts of the business except this one. Forging was the initiating step of our manufacturing process, so somehow, I had to get over my fear of fire. I had to find a way to understand metals and become comfortable with fire's role in molding and shaping them.

What better way to overcome my fear than to face it head-on? In January 2019, I joined a blacksmith class in Texas, the only petite female in a group of largely built burly men. In preparation for class, I found my father's old denim forge apron and took his fireproof gloves with me. Before starting, we were asked what our motivation was for joining. The vast majority alluded to their love for the art of hammering iron and passion for experimenting with fire. With a go-get-'em grin, I confessed, "I'm afraid of fire. Metals are mysterious to me and intimidate me. I'm here to become comfortable with fire and understand how metal behaves with it."

Everyone looked at me with kindness. The instructor shrugged his shoulders and said with a knowing smile, "Ah, you're going to love this."

Under my breath, I muttered, "Dear God, I hope so."

Our first step was to make a fire from coal. The quickest way to accomplish this was to get leftover amber from a neighboring kiln, but I chose to start from nothing. I cleaned the shaft, stacked the coal, and burned some paper for the coal to catch the heat of the flame. I created short gusts of air to fan the flame, and soon, the coals started burning. *Wow! I did it!*

Next, we were instructed to insert a low-alloy iron bar into the fire. Controlling the intensity of fire was critical. If I left the bar in for too long, it would be too soft to hammer. I could tell from its orange-red shade when it was at its optimum state. As I hammered, impurities splattered around, and the bar's core started taking shape the way I wanted. After three days of encountering fire and metal, I was not only comfortable with it, but I also appreciated it.

The life lessons were not lost on me as I shaped the bar through repetition and patience. I could see myself as the metal and recognized the various fires in my life that had shaped me to the core. For metal to be useful, it must go through fire to remove impurities and qualities that don't serve its intended shape. At the right temperature, for the right amount of time, fire enables metal to incorporate other qualities and dimensions to strengthen it further. Fire reveals a metal's unique colors and true purpose.

I had been molded and put through fire more times than I liked—the attack, an unhappy marriage, seeing my children caught in the middle of my divorce, WOM's lawsuit, and losing my beloved brother. Each time, the refining process gave me capabilities I needed for my next phase of growth. The world saw me as a woman, a female. I now saw myself first and foremost as a person.

Feelings of pain, guilt, separation, shame or joy, pride, and confidence come irrespective of gender; they are part of the human experience. As we are like metal, we are also like clay. At birth, we all are just clunky balls of clay to be shaped, molded, and weathered by life to ultimately become our final vessel of purpose. I hold dearly this famous Tao verse: "The shape of a vase takes time and is beautiful, but it is the hollow which makes it useful."

Wise Tides

After my back injury and burn out, I committed to balancing work and fun. In July 2019, my daughters and I traveled to Majorca, Spain, for our annual mother-daughter trip, a special time of bonding, activities, and adventures. On the fifth and final day of our sailing course, we were excited to soon be a certified crew!

Just before heading to the boat, I stepped onto our hotel balcony to soak in the view. As my eyes scanned the horizon over the ocean, taking in the people and sights, I could not help but realize how the world before me was tranquil and in harmony. The wind flowed steady and danced with the white sails of the boats offshore. Water emulated the depth of its own hue, which dazzled turquoise on the surface. On a neighboring hill, the earth synchronized its resources as ripe grapes hung, harvest ready, from the vine and workers prepared an adjacent patch of soil for a new season. The sun's fire served just enough heat for people to tan but not burn while lying on the toasty sands. The space in my heart was boundless with love as I saw people from all parts of the world having fun together, in a moment of an uplifting quietude and grace.

As I held this contentment, my daughters and I packed our gear for the day and headed toward the port to meet our instructors. Joe and Monique were a lovely couple, seasoned in the art of sailing. Their forty-six-foot sailboat was ready with a loaded kitchen and lounge towels in case we stopped to sunbathe on the boat. It always amazed me how the boat had no brakes but could come to a complete stop with a little understanding of the water and air currents.

I looked back at the coast as we cruised away and then gazed forward into the sea. I was in control, at the helm. Today was the grand finale to savor it all. I couldn't help but whistle a tune and tap my foot as the surf gently maneuvered its way. The ship speed was an ideal eight knots. The boat tilted at ninety degrees, and we were on the move. In unison, we jived and tacked our way out of a narrow canal into the sea's magnificence.

As we headed further into the wide-open ocean, land disappeared into the horizon. Gradually, the weather began to change. We had left the perfectly harmonized elements behind. The sun, which just minutes earlier shone brightly, now ducked between clouds as the temperature dropped. The gentle humming breeze increased its pitch, transforming smooth layers of ripples into a top glide of waves.

Before I knew it, we were at twenty-four knots. Our boat then joined the sea's gallop as it tilted high upwards along the choppy curls of water to splash hard twenty feet down, slamming into a pit of another large wave. In seconds, the situation had shifted from tranquil to chaotic. A storm was brewing, pushing us in the wrong direction.

Air howled against both sails. Water currents battled for control of the boat, fighting to get inside. The sail, ropes, and center boom struggled for direction as the wind and water tossed the boat. Monique saw Sharayu sitting at the edge of the boat and quickly called for her to come to the center. The assured energy I'd felt just moments earlier was replaced by concern that consumed my peace. I was not in control anymore; the ocean was. And our ship was in a heated contact sport with the elements.

Right then, Joe shouted over the chaos and restlessness of my mind. "Wow! You three are super special. You get to experience these challenging conditions on your fifth day. You're almost sailors!"

I looked around trying to find who he was talking to. All we wanted was for this to somehow stop and to be back on shore, safe and comfortable. But he was smiling, keeping busy with the ship, having the time of his life.

"Are you ready?" Joe yelled.

"Ready for what?" I shouted. I was about ready to surrender and give up the helm.

Like a head cheerleader, Joe encouraged us again. "We are going to stop and calm this boat. Are you ready?"

I couldn't believe it. The boat didn't have brakes, and clearly the water and air had their own agenda. The optimist I pride myself on being was scared, but it didn't faze Joe. He kept up the motivation as he continued. "All right, now remember everything you've learned. On the count of three, we're going to head straight into the wind."

My eyebrows lifted and my eyes widened. "Straight *into* the wind? You mean face it? Uh, Joe, do you want to take over?"

"Nah, you got this. Just listen to my direction."

Under my breath I whispered, "Um, oookay."

He had more faith in me than I had. In the face of potential danger, my negative thoughts discounted all my efforts and how far I had come.

Merely imagining shore and safety wouldn't get us there. But Bhakti and Sharayu were with me, which meant I had to do everything possible to get us stable. Although I was fearful, with all my might I tapped into my reservoir of faith, hope, and self-trust. It was not easy, but it was the only way forward.

"Okay, Rani, we've got to get control of the boat. Remember, you are at the helm. Keep focused and steer hard to head into the wind. While the boat turns, feel your surroundings to keep the boat balanced. But keep a close eye on the gauges. The instruments will show you reality, whereas the environment might be deceiving." With full focus, my intuition kicked in, and keeping an eye on the pulse of the gauges, I started turning the boat.

Simultaneously, Joe rallied my daughters and Monique toward different ends of the boat to grab the flapping ropes. Together, they pulled in the sails.

Joe cheered. "Okay. Pull in the lines quickly to get the boom straight in the center. We can't have the boom oscillating. It will throw the boat off balance. Once the boom is in the center, the main sail will be firm and work with us to prevent the wind from forcing the boat in a different direction."

I was careful not to steer too drastically, otherwise the boat could have toppled. Working through the angle with prudence, I patiently allowed the boat to adjust. As it lined up with the wind, the front sail, or genoa, started to flutter, and my daughters rolled it in with all their might.

Then Joe announced the next steps. "We have to leave just enough room for the wind to pass through the genoa and flow forward against the mainsail. Both sails will create a boundary with enough resilience and give for the air to pass and the boat to start slowing down with the water. Not too tight, not too loose."

As they adjusted the front sail, the gauges read twelve knots, then eight knots, then four knots. We were actually slowing down! The winds suddenly dropped from a high soprano shrill to a low alto hum. The boat's sideways sway became a front-back rocking.

In his normal yet enthused pitch, Joe called out, "Rani, we're almost there. Gauge readings are looking good. The boat is getting back in control. One last thing now. To slow down the boat even more, let's fire up the engine in reverse. Just a little energy to pull the boat back will help get a complete stop."

I put the throttle in reverse, lifted my head, and looked around. Interestingly, we worked with the turbulence to calm the boat. The water's expanse still reflected a gray warning from the clouds, and the wind still played atop the water, but it was far from entering the boat. As the boat gently adjusted one final time, we glided from a slow cruise to a near stop of less than one knot. No rocking, no gliding, just stable, balanced. Gauges also pointed toward the center and were stable.

We all looked at each other. First in disbelief and then with wide-open smiles. My daughters and I jumped and ran to give Joe and Monique high fives as we all shouted out the loudest victory chant possible. "We did it!"

Right in the middle of our happy dances, Monique announced in her upbeat, yet soothing accent, "What more perfect time to put water on the stove for some tea. You all did great! And I'd say we deserve perfect English biscuits, too. I'll be right back."

As the tea brewed, my daughters and I sat around the boat to take it all in. An overwhelming joy bubbled inside, yet we were speechless, in admiration of all we'd accomplished. My mind quieted and I was in awe. I played back the roller-coaster ride of all I had just witnessed. We'd learned to work with the characteristics of the turbulence to overcome it until we were in harmony with the elements around us. We could coexist in the same space. It was an incredible experience.

In our silence, I heard the gentle drops of tea pouring into our ceramic cups. I took a sip and voiced a bit of my curiosity. "Joe, how were you so calm and collected when everything around you was chaotic?"

He looked up and thought for a second. "When I sail across the Atlantic for weeks, there are times when the seas become unstable, just like we experienced. In those moments, I consciously do a few things. You see, it can get crazy out there, but here," Joe pointed to his head, "I control that, and I don't let the crazy in there. The real power I have is in my thoughts and actions." He poured another cup of tea. "First, I stop and hone in on my thoughts. Next, I look around to get a sense of direction, of where I am and where I need to go. Then, I review my map to check for any course changes needed. Once I mark the next move in my head, I'm ready to continue. Oh, I forgot one step. I will have a cup of tea, and then continue," he said with a gregarious laugh.

I took it all in, making mental notes of the sailor's wisdom.

A couple of hours later, we gallantly sailed toward our home port as the sun set with vibrant colors over the mountains. What a ride, figuratively and practically. Our instructors proudly signed our sailing certificates. For my daughters and I, it was more than just a paper. It was a memory and a moment of victory in which the elements worked in harmony with power for peace. A lesson none of us would ever forget.

In storms, you may feel like nothing makes sense, like your aspirations and dreams have come to an end, that your plan has failed and there is no hope. That is the time to tap into memories of faith and endurance. Remember the times you overcame difficulties.

When you go through a difficult situation, there are things around you that need to be protected so they can grow and live out their purpose. There are qualities within you that become your resources, and you must be aware of what you are capable of and what the people around you are capable of. Be sensitive and empathetic, especially during a storm, so as not to leave anyone behind. Be aware of who is around you, and who you are responsible for.

Remember you are here. You got "here" for a reason, and you will get "there" in the proper time. No one can box you in and tell you who you are or what you deserve. The moment you look within to the open-ness of your mind and heart, you see possibility, and you realize there is more. Knowing there is enough shatters the barriers.

Accept the opportunities in the storm to better yourself. Allow the elements of life to work with you and to love you. Every boat must carry itself, make its own space, and make its own way. When you stand up for yourself, everything around you will fall into place. The storms, people, and problems are just trying to find their own balance, and your intersection with them creates the space to grow, love, and to find a new way.

Untitled

April 12, 2021
Mallorca, Spain

Ride the wave!
As it lifts with the swell
Of the ocean's miracle.
Question not its time
Nor manage its interval.

Go! Ride! Surf!
What may come.
For the rise orchestrated
Your glide, your vision.

Crest begins to rumble
After years of silent tugs.
How far and deep
Had I traveled
To prepare for this lift above.

Only those of balance
Walking earth and flying sky
Keep focus to experience one.

Where waves are wings
And breath is light,
The waiting shore
Is greater than the sum!

The Bond Between Mom and Daughter

After all life had shown me, and the events that had shaped who I had become, I was ready to be my best and serve my purpose for all those around me. First, I chose to serve my parents, as their daughter.

Watching parents age is probably one of the hardest changes for a child to witness. I've learned to adapt to their needs, to empathize with their fears of days coming soon, and to relate to an undeniable truth that one day I will be there as well. Lessons of love have been revealed to me while caring for my aging mother through her struggles with Parkinson's disease, where love was the only power to see her through one of the hardest times for her and our family.

In August 2020, the coronavirus global pandemic was still unraveling and had been since March of that year. Governments and people around the world tried to navigate unprecedented work, family, and social norms. The day both India and the US announced, almost simultaneously, that their borders were closing is one I will never forget. At first, I wasn't sure how serious this was. However, the news and airlines made the seriousness clear with a slew of canceled flights and only a handful available for those who wanted to quickly return home.

At that time, Bhakti was with me in Pune, as I prepared for two major global events: Impact India, our foundation's global-service leadership program through the Puranik Foundation, followed by WOM's bi-annual summit two weeks later. To add to that, this book was to debut in Pune. In an instant, everything changed. Upon learning the borders would soon close, I had to drop everything and redirect my focus.

At 4:00 a.m., I contacted a very sleepy and tired Sharayu and instructed her to exit France, cutting short her study abroad program for the spring semester at Grenoble University, so she could make it back to Houston on one of the last flights out of Europe, which eventually would reopen after an uncertain five months. Bhakti and I needed to leave India so we could all be together in Houston. If there was anything the three of us knew by then, it was that, in times of uncertainty, if we were together, we could handle anything that came our way.

Thankfully, although my dad typically travels three or four times each year, he had been in Houston since February. That left mom alone in Pune, so I called and asked her to come with us. Very calmly she said, "Oh, don't worry. I still have my schoolchildren here, and we will figure it out either way. I don't want to go there. I have nothing to do there. Besides, if things really do shut down, I can get more work done at the foundation site."

There was no arguing with her. The school was her happy place, and she was surrounded by nearly fifty permanent staff members and additional help if needed. If only I'd known the loneliness and depression she would suffer through a very odd and challenging isolation from the world, I wouldn't have given her a choice. Within two weeks, she had to close the school and send all the children home, except for a handful whose parents lived too far away and who missed the window before public transportation shut down.

As the weeks and months passed, our home was full with Bhakti, Sharayu, and me, along with our two rescue dogs, Sox and Beans. We decided to use the time wisely, so we spent most of March doing a deep clean of the house, organizing, redecorating, and downsizing in every area we could. Over a six-week period, we completed a three-thousand-piece puzzle of an African wildlife safari. We binge-watched shows. We danced, cooked, cleaned, and talked deeply about the changing face of the world and the call of Mother Earth. We spoke as daughters of a wise and eternal mother who was calling out for balance and harmony.

We shared our views of what was expected of us as daughters of this planet, as humans of this living existence. We took note of what we were doing to be environmentally aware, and then we devised additional actions to take in an effort to heal this hurting planet. Save water, recycle, buy only what is needed, respect food, eat enough for our body but no more, love nature, and most importantly, love all people. Support all those in need, give more of our talents and our time. Be empathetic and do what we can to ease hurt, and be cheerful and of good, positive faith to attract good health for all.

Through April and May, Mom took on loads of work, organizing, cleaning, and supervising small construction projects. We spoke by phone at least twice a week, and all seemed okay. She was proud of all she and her team had accomplished despite the blazing summer heat typical of those two months in Pune.

Then came June. She was exhausted, had extremely low energy, and was waiting desperately for the monsoon rain clouds to burst life-nourishing drops from the sky. Food was becoming difficult to get. Farms had dried up in surrounding villages. Whatever grains they had on campus, the staff and remaining students shared and essentially ate to fill their bellies, but there was nothing exciting about the daily staples of the same rice and grains. Each day, as the food stores diminished little by little, worry crept in.

Mom would normally fly from Pune to Houston every four to five months. Now, with a travel ban, she began to miss Houston and feel the distance, even with our twice-weekly calls. Social distancing and the global lockdown created the eerie feeling of losing one's freedom. For my mother, this distance and relative solitude also brought on a debilitating depression. By July, she fell ill and shared that she was feeling very weak. She didn't even have the energy to get up and was not interested in doing anything. She didn't want to eat or sleep. She was simply existing.

Around mid-July, when I called to check on her, from the strained tone of her voice, I could tell she had a lot on her mind, but she didn't say much. With every call, she grew quieter. By the end of July, she had been hospitalized twice. The first hospitalization was for digestive issues, and she was back home in four days. The second hospitalization was for the same reason, but this time the issue had escalated. From this point, her health took a nosedive.

With college campuses reopening, I dropped Sharayu back at her dorm in Georgetown in early August. Through all the challenges of COVID-19, I was grateful for six months together with my daughters. We were emotionally more resilient and spiritually focused on the quality of our lives and making a positive difference to all lives. Through it all, three words rang strong—patience, grace, and vision—and they became my guiding principles to overcome all emotional challenges.

Patience: All works out in the grand plan. My job is to allow the situation to unfold so it can live its journey.

Grace: We all deserve slack, to give ourselves space to empathize, to tap into the truth that no one has the right answer, and we all are trying our best, even when others behave as if they know it all.

Vision: Faith to see beyond reminds me that a current challenge is a temporary stage or moment and there is a much bigger plan and purpose.

On the way back home from Georgetown, I casually called my sister and mom, only to discover my mother was still in the hospital. I knew there was more to her illness than anyone had told me, more than Mom understood. As soon as the call ended, I had the strongest feeling ever, an urgency from the life-force core of my belly that only a mother would know. The pain of losing a sibling or a friend, which only a sister would fathom, rushed through my blood. I felt a fire in the deepest and most secret parts of my being where I hid gratitude and love for my parents. Only a daughter would understand an ailing mother's cry for help.

Even though the world was locked down, I had to leave as soon as possible to be with Mom. She wouldn't say it, but she was homesick and there was much more to it. She was lonely, and worse, she was dealing with the haunting loneliness, guilt, helplessness, and sadness that came with memories of her son, who had died in the month of August, the same month both he and she were born, just one week and thirty-eight years apart.

She needed her family. It was time for me to be a mother to my own mother. She had been my best *Sesame Street* singing buddy, my friend, always. I knew I was to be a sister to my best friend, to listen to her and help her live. I was to shower her with love with no rhyme or reason, just because she was my mother and I loved her. The fearless woman in me arose, assertive and focused, knowing I had to go and be with her. Even in the midst of a global pandemic, I would find a way to be with my mother.

How time opened up for me was incredible. That very day, I booked the earliest flight out of Houston, which was ten days later. I had to take my COVID test within a certain timeframe and upload numerous documents for approval to fly out of the US and to be accepted by India's government to fly in.

Five days before my flight, India opened its borders to all OCI card holders (a visa card for people with origins in India). I didn't need to wait for a special pass or bubble flight to India. Three days later, the Indian government further relaxed regulations for international travelers. People who had a residence in India could home-quarantine for fourteen days as long as they got prior approval. This meant I didn't have to quarantine in a registered hotel for fourteen days any longer. My journey became less complicated by the day. This was a demonstration for me of God parting the seas.

As soon as I landed in India, I went straight home to Mom with a bag full of croissants, hot sauce, chips, tortillas, iceberg lettuce, and her favorite pizza from Houston. The moment we reunited, we hugged—mine the desperate, relieved hug of a concerned child, hers the weak embrace of an elderly, ill parent, still very much pleased to see me. The first faint words out of her frail body were, *"Tujhi koop vat pahili ga. Khoop vat pahili.* I've been waiting so long for you, dear, so long."

My soul ached at hearing those words. I thought, *Why haven't you told me this before?* She sounded like she was carrying the shadow of death. Her eyes were sunken, and she was very pale. She had zero energy. Still, I rejoiced that I was with her now. The little girl, who grew to know the heart of a mother, was now grown up and a mother in my own right, yet I was still her cub. As my daughters have done for me, I stepped up to protect my lifelong lioness. She needed me now.

The next morning was my late brother's birthday. By then, grief had taken over every one of my mother's cells. She couldn't get up from her bed, but I was determined we would celebrate. I was his sister, and now, like a sister to Mom. I put music on and danced in her room and around the premises with all the remaining staff. Soon, the energy shifted, and a spirit of laughter and happy memories of my brother surfaced. We all spoke about him, and I pretended to joke with him saying, "Mahesh, you must be having fun up there, knowing we all are celebrating your birthday with your favorite cake. Don't worry. We'll finish it all on your behalf."

I was Mom's sister and confidante, the one who knew the small nuances of our growing up and the stresses and pleasures of being raised together. I understood her line of authority but could take responsibility in a heartbeat. We laughed for no reason and had a profound instance of overwhelming crying, the kind where siblings often feel safer to let go with each other than with a parent.

For the first two weeks, Mom needed to be nursed back to health. I worked with her, understanding the changing nature and needs of a woman's body. It was hard for her to accept the changes in her physicality, which offered more restrictions and helplessness than energy or vitality did. She tried to adjust to her new form and abilities, but she became frustrated and even disheartened. This was not about anyone saying she could or could not do something; it was a harsh reality of aging. Throughout various stages of life, we all face drastic, never-before-experienced changes. When we realize time cannot be rewound, we are forced to accept and live with the alterations, happily or unhappily.

Eventually Mom began to recover, and we switched roles between daughter and mother to best serve and support her through each circumstance. The constants in each role were love, kindness, and forgiveness, plus everything I learned during COVID. Being the firstborn, unknowingly and humbly, I set a precedent for the younger siblings and the next generations, putting family first and being brave, courageous, caring, giving, and loving.

Shubhangi, Bhakti, and I shared the responsibility of caring for Mom. We rotated our time with her so someone from the family would continuously be with her for the next three months. After six weeks of undivided attention and dedication to her, it was time for me to return to Houston. Mom now had reliable health and home staff. She gracefully and confidently zipped around in her motorized wheelchair. Her school and property staff were organized with schedules, targets to achieve, zones to manage, cameras, and walkie-talkies. Mom could practically control and command anything she desired on campus with a simple click. She even learned how to use video calling and watch church online. She was back!

My Father's Daughter

I returned to Houston in September 2020. Dad and I had planned a quiet and private sit-down. The thought of *lessons of leadership* ran through my consciousness. My father, mentor, and role model was preparing to hand over the company, his dream, his love that he created forty years earlier, to his child, his daughter, Rani. It was a tremendous honor.

To ensure his vision was protected, I had done everything within my ability to grow the company with his fundamental principles intact, and I assured him I would continue that objective. I asked him to share his expectations of me and what values and business culture he wanted to see passed on for generations to come. This was important to me. Having operated my own dance company, ISHA, in India for fourteen years, I knew the heart connection of care and passion to start a business, to work with people, and to witness the growth and success of a company. I also knew the pain of ending something so dear to me, which had great potential, all due to my inability to serve it and the absence of a legacy plan to take it forward.

He was the founder of his legacy. I was the next in line. For my role to be successful, I had to respect the roots of the company and be a catalyst for the new and expanding branches of the future. I promised him I would support all his desires while taking his dream and vision beyond his lifetime. At seventy-six years old, his age at the time of this writing, my father continues to exude youthful energy and a lively spirit. He sincerely believes his playground is research and development. The WOM shop is his happy place, where challenges can be resolved and genius solutions can turn his vision into reality

Our conversation began slowly, easily, warmly, as we discussed his heartfelt belief that the secret to good health is good food. Over a healthy lunch of soup and salad, we discussed Mom's well-being, his health, and my ever-adapting food preferences, which tended to change with new nutrition science or my evolving mind-body balance. We toasted with glasses of orange juice to how things panned out for Mom and to his feeling strong, alert, and excited about life. These things mattered in the grand scheme of our broader conversation about legacy.

A few months earlier, I'd learned an Indian author was writing a book about my father in Marathi, later to be translated into English. "So, Dad," I said, "how do you feel about the book being written about your life and leadership philosophies? We should list your top ten leadership principles and focus on your inspirational journey 'from nothing to nothing is impossible.'"

He nodded shyly, and then he looked straight at me and said, "You're forgetting something."

"What is that, Baba?"

"We have to include *your* story."

I paused to allow myself a moment of admiration for him. He never thought only of himself but made sure to give everyone around him credit first. Still, I hadn't expected this response. "Baba, this is *your* story. *Your* legacy."

"Yes, but it would be incomplete without people understanding your role in it. What you have done for the company, no one else could have done," he stated sincerely; the words echoed like the sound of a cardinal singing on a warm spring morning. "You've taken this company in a new direction of growth. You have a clear vision, and your hard work is being watched by all. When people see me, they now see you. They are watching you as the next in line, and I can tell you there is so much respect for the way you are leading."

I didn't know what to do except smile and say, "I'm your daughter, Baba. It's all from you. I cannot be any other way."

With a level of warmth and emotion I had not seen or felt in all my years, he gently spoke. "Yes, you are."

I usually don't tear up, but this was something the little girl inside had dreamed of for decades. I'd long since made peace with how things were with my father and me. Yet, in this moment, I took it all in. A physical shift overwhelmed me. I felt overjoyed and full of love as these words from the father, whose DNA flowed through me, came to life and swirled through all my cells. Our emotions were looped like a magnetic field full of energy, purpose, and love.

"Rani, you know my heart. It is in innovation and creation of products. But I tell you this with all my sincerity. If ever I get in your way, if I am a hindrance to where you want to take this company, you just have to tell me. I'll be out of your way."

My gasp was one of astonishment, the highest respect, and an unyielding understanding of who he was. He was a partner who led by respecting and appreciating his co-supporters, those who made even the most minuscule success possible. He was not only watching me, but he was also watching others. He was ready to protect and proclaim my role, as a lion would, in the midst of the unknown. He led with direct honesty in what he had to say and with trust that we would have each other's back, no matter what. He was leading *me* so I could lead *others*.

I was a girl, a woman, his daughter, and his firstborn child. And he was so proud. He understood what that meant in society, in our industry, and he wanted to make a difference, to prove all humans are equal. In 2016, the same year I was promoted to Global CFO, he established a scholarship and appreciation fund for working women at WOM who excelled in their field. He proudly named it the Indu Puranik Foundation, after his mother.

My father's journey and the lessons he learned along the way all flashed before me in an instant. As I sat admiring him, he continued to embrace changes as the world changed around him. Not only did he conceptually incorporate new ways, but he also acted on them in his own life to be his best self and to serve at his best all others around him. One fundamental leadership quality he held constant through every change was to lead with grace and humility.

"Baba," I murmured, pausing to gather my thoughts. "Baba, you are my role model. I know I've never said this. You are. What you just said, no one says. No creator, no founder, no person of authority ever had the courage or heart to say it, but you did. You are so much bigger than you know. God must be looking at you as one of His favorite children. I know He is. Baba, I promise you, when it is time for me to hand over the torch to the next leader, I will say the same. If ever I am in the way of the next growth, I will step away in a heartbeat with the same grace you have shown me."

And so, we began our next chapter. One in which father and daughter connected on many dimensions and with a purpose for him to teach and for me to carry his wisdom further into the years, well beyond his lifetime and mine.

"Baba, what is your vision for the company?" I asked.

He explained certain aspects of the company that led to his success, such as innovating technologically and always offering a quality, high-technology product. He beamed as he explained how, where, and why the company could expand in particular industries. Amazed at his forward thinking, I asked which values were close to his heart that he would want to see as a legacy for the company.

"Dignity," he said without a second thought. "Always give people dignity, no matter what they may have done. We will never know what caused a person to behave or react a certain way," he explained. "We have no authority to judge. Always treat others with dignity. Also, remember that loyalty cannot be substituted. Remain loyal to your customers, to your service, and to what you have to offer. Never change that. Never shortchange anybody. Being loyal, as a company, is who we are."

My attention hung on every word he spoke. The light in his eyes was bright as he explained his philosophy for success.

"Remember all the people who have helped you become successful," he said. "You know this well, but always give people credit. The success of a company is never due to one person; it is a team of people. Treat them well. It's okay to give more because it will eventually come back to you in multitudes, either in this life or the next. Keep a good heart and everything else will come."

I shut my eyes and nodded for a few brief seconds, taking it all in. There was silence between us, a silence which crossed time and tied all loose ends, an infinity bond.

He then asked, "What is your vision?"

I had been toying with ideas of innovation and technology to further develop current strengths and assets of the company using tools and processes that would allow us to continue specializing in what we do best. My outlook was to scale, to partner with institutions that could foster our vision and growth. I told him I wanted to enhance our human capabilities for creativity and innovation and development and to find new ways of using automation to enhance the capabilities of people.

"Like you, Baba, I believe people come first. That means we must strive for work-life quality, along with a high-product quality, which is designed and produced with optimal efficiency."

He grew excited and loved all the ideas. He looked at me in the certain way he has, and I knew he was pleased. "That's the way to go, Rani. Start right away, and I know you'll make it happen."

"Let's do this, Baba," I said with a smile.

We spoke for another two hours, dreamt about the future, and reminisced about his WOM journey. We spoke of gratitude to God for choosing us to be His messengers, and we parted with a promise to eternally be obedient to Him.

In December 2020, my father officially asked me to take over the company. We didn't want to make a formal announcement. Instead, we wanted WOM's people to see the transition organically over time. The work we both did would continue irrespective of the formal positions we held. It took a week to sign all the paperwork, and we completed the process the day before shooting a documentary, inside our company headquarters, for the BBC. *American Dream* shares stories of immigration and building a legacy here in the US. God's timing is always impeccable.

After the filming was complete, my father and I stood up to say our goodbyes. He was leaving for India the next morning. This would be the last time I would see him until he visited Houston again. The next time we would see each other, I would be EVP and incoming CEO of WOM. As we hugged, I recognized this as one of life's bittersweet moments. As he slowly drove past me and Bhakti, he said, "Bye." With one word, I was transported back to the feeling of being the three-year-old girl, the daughter who fought internally for approval, the child who had to say bye to her father every morning as he dropped her off at day care, wondering when he would pick her up to take her home.

Then, a fullness washed over me, a deep peace, a contentment and satisfaction. Our relationship was complete; all had been journeyed and learned. Not only was I *his* daughter, but I was *a* daughter, a child with unique traits and gifts only a female could experience. It was incredibly emotional for me, but I did not have time to savor those emotions. With the filming complete, we still had to clean up, and I needed to pull myself together. I wiped my face and said a quick prayer of gratitude. As I turned to exit the WOM office building, something shifted yet again.

It was time to say goodbye to the little girl within.

I took a deep breath and opened the door.

I was free.

Hands Changing

December 13, 2020
9:24 p.m., Houston, Texas

My hands look tougher
Rugged edges, older.
Steady they are
To uphold morals,
Relentless work ethic
Lifting burdens.

When I clasp them
The Lord's strength
Feels evident.
Wise, bold, courageous,
Their lock firmly
Rests my head in prayer.

Soothing, soft,
Innocently free
Evolved quietly . . .
To diligently be.

Pursue your calling,
Let age not betray.
Your mind will pair
The hands to make a way.

Run no more, for your lines speak
Of commitment
Of dedication
Of anything but weak.

FINAL COUNTDOWN

"It ain't over till it's over."
~ Yogi Berra

The simplest, most freeing lesson was waiting patiently for forty-nine years to reveal itself: the true purpose of life. The very question that fundamentally rooted my search to making sense of life finally revealed itself to me. I had been in India for four months, having planned a six-month visit to focus entirely on WOM India. Since 2016, I had meticulously worked with other WOM locations to standardize, streamline, and restructure. In 2021, India was the final piece of the puzzle and the most critical. WOM's largest manufacturing footprint was in Pune with over 2,500 people. All production started there, and it was the foundation to realizing WOM's growth and expansion as I envisioned.

This would be a difficult, long stay away from my daughters, as well as my chosen family and friends. My routine shifted to a completely different working style in India, beginning and ending later in the day. This was a test of how I juggled work between time zones and daylight-savings adjustments. After a full workday in the office, I had calls with the US teams, often until midnight.

I was still trying my best to fix things for both my parents and find ways to make their lives easier, more meaningful, and more joyous. Of course, they could handle their own lives; this was just my full heart to care and serve. Or so I thought. In reality, this was a remnant of my inherent need to please. In Pune, Dad and I always worked together and had lengthy discussions on current issues, finding solutions and planning for the future. During this trip, however, Dad's knee troubles were more severe. He'd experienced knee pain for the past few years, and by now, things were getting worse. In addition, in March 2021, Mom's school had to shut down again due to the second strong wave of COVID.

Both my parents had made certain choices in their lives that resulted in their state of unfulfilled desires. Often, they reminisced and verbalized their wish to have family around. Dad would say, "We are all so far apart, doing our own things. What happened to the simple joys of bonding and family interactions? I miss that very much."

My mind went into fix-it mode. *What can I do? Should I stay with Dad while I'm in India, or should I visit mom at her school a little more often in between my crazy work schedule?* My conclusion: Take a step back; I couldn't do it.

In April 2021, on Good Friday, I was meditating when my still inner voice bubbled up a phrase I was surprised to hear. "Release your parents."

My eyes popped wide open. *What did that even mean? How could I do that? Why would I want that?* As these initial thoughts quieted, that inner voice repeated, *"Release your parents."* This phrase kept swirling in my mind for a day before the meaning was revealed. It meant releasing the bondage of my childhood expectations along with the burdens I had placed on myself to be responsible for this phase of their lives. I could help, but I could not take ownership of what they needed to feel fulfilled. I had to be okay with putting myself first, and loving myself first, so I could love my parents, my children, and anyone else, without the need to fix them. I understood.

As I moved away from fear, closer to freedom, I basked in this new awareness of fearlessness. I began speaking up for my values, gently, humbly, and respectfully, but affirmatively. Years of unspoken topics about family and work all presented themselves to be addressed. Years of silence and layers of unspoken conversations began to shed. At the other end of the release was the receiving of who I am, in totality. I loved me, what I had become, how I became, and the direction I was heading in.

This began what I consider the final countdown to the conclusion of my last, or seventh cycle. There were twenty-one days until April 24th, my birthday, and something miraculous was about to happen. I could feel it. My book was not yet finished. The upcoming days had to reveal my last and final lesson before the book would be complete. I planned a short visit to the Himalayas, as a birthday treat for me. I needed solitude to reflect, and I quite simply needed a date with God, to recharge and enjoy nature's rhythm without the confines or demands of man-made time. Those well-laid plans were changed one week before my birthday.

On April 14th, Dad said, "We're going to Houston on the twenty-first. Let's get tickets before COVID gets too serious. I've received my second dose of the vaccine, so there is no reason to wait any longer."

It seemed as if whenever Dad or Mom needed me, I just picked up and left. Was anyone aware of the constant sacrifices I made to accommodate everyone? Instead of brewing silently, I spoke up, making sure they understood how I felt. Once I had stated my thoughts and feelings about the interruption of my plans, I took a moment to consider my dad's suggestion. Considering the uncertainty of COVID, I concluded he was right; we should return to Houston. It was the right thing to do, but such a heartbreak for me. My rendezvous with God was canceled.

In preparation for departure from India, I had to complete two months of planned work in record time. An unstoppable rush overtook me. Three to four hours of sleep was enough to get me powered up to tackle my list of the major assignments I had to complete before my departure. I felt a sense of urgency and a feeling of obedience to wrap up everything, leaving no lingering thoughts or tasks to carry forward. Within a week, I completed my main task in India, releasing budgets for WOM's India and Houston locations. With that, I had planted a seed for the company's legacy. The final note to the symphony of WOM's restructuring for growth was written and harmoniously orchestrated.

I was ready to go home. Not to celebrate my birthday in solitude, but to be surrounded by the love of my close friends and family and to celebrate with my children, all my children, the two daughters who were born *from* me and the many daughters and sons who were born *for* me. I was going home two days before touching the finish line of forty-nine, and not by myself, but with my parents.

I'd always felt I should have been born in Houston rather than in India. This seemingly small pivot on my mother's part had the biggest impact during the most testing times of my life. Now, I was returning to the country where I was supposed to be birthed and to the soil I was supposed to be planted in. What better way for God to show His divine orchestration than to cancel my very date with Him and have me travel from Pune to Houston with both my parents for the first time in my entire life? This was a sign that my pilgrimage was over, my suffering was over, and the lessons from challenges I'd experienced throughout my life were understood. It felt like a rebirth.

During our layover in Dubai, while sitting in the airport lounge, my mother made the same observation.

"Rani, we are taking you home. You are being born again," she said.

"Really, Mom, you saw this too?" I asked.

She nodded, and I explained to her my concept of seven-year cycles, that we are literally made new after each one.

On that, Dad chimed in. Little did I know that he and I shared the same thoughts on this topic. "Absolutely," he said. "Did you know I just completed my eleventh chapter. So yes, I believe you, and I too have seen distinct roles I've played every seven years."

During our flight, I checked in with mom who was sitting just behind me. She was lying flat with tears streaming down her face. I sat next to her and gently asked, "What's going on, Mom, what are you thinking of?"

She struggled to utter words. "I'm homesick," she finally said.

It hadn't even been twenty-four hours since we left India. There was more going on than that. "What do you mean?"

She gave a somber reply. "I feel like this even when I'm in India. What is the purpose of all this?"

I looked around to see what, if anything, had triggered her flood of emotions. On the TV screen, a movie, *Illegal*, told the story of an immigrant coming to the United States and portrayed his initial days of struggle.

"Like in that movie," Mom explained. "It reminded me of my first time in the US. Nothing was easy, none of it made sense, and it still doesn't. We do things, we keep busy, and we search for freedom and happiness. Why do we do it all?"

At first, I did not know how to answer the profundity of this question because this was the exact question I had been asking myself. I was being asked what it truly means to be free. My spiritual quest, which began as a young girl, had been a search for identity, purpose, and meaning. The underlying curiosity to answer this mystery had always been driven by a desire to understand most deeply what it means to be free.

Over the course of many years, many lessons, and my personal evolutions, I'd had different definitions of freedom. At times, I thought it was being able to soar high or to do anything at will. As a child, freedom was to explore my creativity without anyone's approval. As a sister, freedom was to be available to protect and guide my siblings when I felt I could give them better. As a lady, freedom was to rebel against discrimination at the cost of my own true choice. As a mother, freedom was to help others find their voice even though I was scared to apply the same for myself. As a wife, freedom was to love unconditionally and be okay with self-depletion. As a woman, freedom was to fight to accept my identity and surrender to loneliness to protect my values. As a daughter, freedom was to dig through layers of cultural barriers to let my faith rise. What was the connecting thread in my journey?

Honestly, as complex and interconnected as the maze was, for me to realize the answer to it all was simple yet casually profound.

Freedom is to live.

As long as I live, I have the ability to make choices, to decide what is next. I'd been chasing freedom in every cycle of my life, and through trial, error, hardship, and love, it was in the living that I was free. Not surviving or letting others or a situation choose over me, but fully living. I saw three distinct pathways to living fully: love, leadership, and legacy. Integrating love always guided me to lead myself and others. This way of leading has become my legacy.

Looking back at each juncture in my journey, it was with great appreciation and deep gratitude that I came to understand my life's challenges and the lessons within them. Freedom is living, simply living. When I live, I am free. I have felt it in every cell of my body, mind, and spirit.

Now, I needed to carefully articulate this to Mom. Pausing to collect my thoughts, I quietly prayed for words to flow through me and offer healing and a sense of peace and understanding to her. In that moment, I felt a wave surge from within. As I inhaled deeply, the words emanated with a calm, universal resolve. In reality, I too listened to those words. They revealed the most valuable lesson and the grand finale to not only my seventh chapter, but to my entire life to that point. Why do we do what we do and what is it all for?

"You know Mamaji, *Aapan anandacha shodhak asto, paan ananda aplyala shodhat asta.*" (We are looking for happiness, but happiness is looking for us.) Isn't it interesting to observe that each time we feel joy or share something meaningful, or when we see someone's eyes light up, it makes us happy? There's an unspoken connection, an exchange of positive energy, a burst of light merging from each other making the atmosphere brighter. We even feel lighter, less heavy or weighed down. We can either be light or darkness; there's no in between. And what is light? Light is love. Light is life. Light or love lives within us and all around us. It is living! And in its living it is free. That freedom is what makes us happy!

Happy is love, light unattached, unconditional, without any expectation of return, without judgment or constraint. We see light every day, but light never asks, 'What's the meaning of all this? What's my purpose?'

"Plants take what they need, animals use it, and humans benefit from it however they want. Light is a constant; it never changes its intensity. Light and love don't need to choose to live. They just are, eternally present, available, absolute, free!

"As humans, as physical beings with free will, it is up to us to choose light, to choose love, to experience it. This is possible only when we live. That's why the only thing that makes sense to me, through all the chaos and crazy, is that when we live, we are free. We cannot keep freedom for just ourselves. That would be like trying to keep light confined in a single container. It will always find a way out and be free."

I knew I was talking a lot, so I stopped and smiled at Mom.

She looked so beautiful. Her wisdom, her curiosity, her love to keep learning and growing. It was more than age or looks. It was a feeling.

I hugged her ever so gently and said in her ear, "I guess the beauty of freedom, of living, is to love it all and watch it expand."

Mom looked into my eyes and gently held my hand. I got goosebumps as I felt her energy, her abundant love. It was like the way she looked at me when I was a baby. Her love was overflowing, gentle, and peaceful as she whispered to me, "Suunnny days . . . sweepin' up . . . hmmm, hmmm, hmmm . . ." My heart felt her light, her freedom, her life.

I kissed her hands, and she closed her eyes.
It all came together.
Freedom.

Freedom

April 24, 2021
8:24 a.m., Houston, Texas

Freedom
As light in day
Embrace me
In every way.

See your tomorrow
Grace, love, and joy
Windswept laughter
Bounties set forth.

I am who
Was made complete
To live, to fly,
To reach the peak.

But now, no search
No wonder of where
I am here
I am life
I am free as air.

Send the light
Beyond my touch
As I step with you
Being your torch.

Lessons learned
Crafted me well
Now I'm free
Ready to tell.

Hope is not a wish

But partners me.
Love is not unknown
As it lives in me.

Stories will be told
Journey deep and wide
Wings of heaven
In freedom I ride.

Be light
So it stays light
Brilliance
Or silence
It carries through the night.

Be of peace
As I've been blessed
Watch His glory
In living and rest.

Free am I
In who the light shines
Everlasting
In love of the Divine.

Rani

Dearest Daughters,

Oh, this seventh phase! What a ride! Just when you thought you were on your way, you suddenly dealt with one curve ball and then another hit hard, relentless. Oh, the anger and frustrations and sheer fatigue of the fight. I know you were so looking for a break, just a little breather. And when you got it, your body wouldn't support you like before. It was entering its own phase and began asking for your attention. I'm so sorry you had to go through this. I would just close my eyes and pray it all to be done already.

I wish it was easy and we could just depend on at least our body taking us through. Oh dearest, how quickly we take our body for granted and assume it will always be intact while enduring. It's not a machine. It has its own language, its own life cycles. So you had to be bold and learn to love all the changes. Life stretched you and broke you to where you didn't think you would ever find the pieces of you. You questioned and doubted whether there was love in any of it.

Well, Love is in the connections, the connection between old and new, between every change and shift, between the living and ones passed on. Love holds all of you, every piece of you like a bridge and connects you to life and living it. It's in this connection, your divine connection, that you learned it is safe to let go. This is your superpower, to let go! And you did it. How beautifully your life started coming together, easier, simpler. You knew well to not give up, to never let go, and to keep believing in Love's connection. Now check you out! You are starting to look up again and have a playfulness and a lightness about you.

This feeling of light is Love and is the secret connector to legacy. Only Love lasts. Only Love could lead you to go further in the toughest, most heartbreaking matters. Only Love keeps the peace yet connects you firmly to where you need to go and the decisions you must make. Only Love connects who you are today to who you can be tomorrow and who you are meant to touch far beyond your physical lifetime.

So go ahead, shout! Shout at the top of your lungs. You did it! You rose above. You made it through it all! Everything came together, one day, one phase, one life at a time.

Now, live. Live fully, my dearest. Now you know, there is always a way to choose, to live, to love.

There is always a way to live playfully, powerfully, and purposefully

Love always,
Rani

THE END IS THE BEGINNING
AGE FORTY-NINE AND BEYOND

"You don't get to live twice."
~ Zindagi Na Milegi Dobara

My Dear Daughters and Sons,
 Many times in the past I've been asked, "So what role will you play next after your 7X7?" I couldn't answer then, but I expected I would know after I'd gone through my seventh phase. In recent days, the answer came. I am complete. I am free. Now, all the lessons to be learned and shared will be learned and shared in freedom.

My blessing to you is for you to discover your lessons in each of your chapters. We all have them. Mine were dominated by my gender and spiritual quest. Yours will be uniquely and wonderfully different, tailor-made for you.

It is amazing how many lessons are available to us if we only take the time to notice, acknowledge, and reflect on them. The universe offers us much wisdom and answers all questions. We only have to be willing to ask, to look, to listen, and to learn. In this way, we have the power to choose and to be free. But here's the catch. Freedom comes with responsibility—responsibility to avoid being overridden by negativity, *guilt, insecurity, dependencies, jealousy, or fear; responsibility to never encroach on anyone else's freedom.*

My greatest hope for this book—these letters from my heart—is that it allows you to see some of those lessons and begin thinking about them in the context of your own life. Every lifetime and every situation provides an opportunity for learning. More than anything else, I wanted to share some of what my life lessons have given me in hopes that perhaps your journey could be easier, and you could learn without going through some hard parts.

Now, at the age of fifty, I am far from done. I eagerly await my future and the turn of the next cycle. I don't know what it will bring me, but I am filled with a calm anticipation. All the ages of my life have been rich and valuable. I am now certain in my purpose, ready to go where God is leading me.

I do not consider myself an authority on anything other than my own life, but if you will allow me to play the role of the teacher, the elder, or the trusted caregiver, only for a moment, I have something to offer you.

My prayer for you, all the persons of this world, all the sons and daughters is this: May you allow yourself to laugh through the hardest times; seek light through the darkness; be kind yet assertive; appreciate your journey and receive love; keep things simple; and most vitally, know that you always have a choice, and there is always a way to live light-full and love-filled.

With love, laughter, and light,
Rani

ACKNOWLEDGMENTS

I am sincerely grateful for all the wonderful beings of light around me and for their support, encouragement, and words of wisdom as I wrote this book. I am also deeply thankful to all those I have mentioned throughout these pages. From the tiniest moment, season, or grand life that I have been a part of, each person has enriched my journey and inspired me to continue discovering my best self and to share my learning as I go.

My editor, Anita Henderson, the quintessential book whisperer. My WOM team, whom I consider my immortal family going out two hundred years and which defines a new dimension of leadership each year. My Puranik Foundation core, Leslie Ausucua.

My EA, friend, and number one, Roxana Arroyo, who kept everything on time and in line, sprinkled the perfect amount of sunshine when needed, and protected my time with exquisite balance. My parents, Rekha and Sudhir Puranik, to whom my respect and love cannot be expressed enough. To Homer Garza, my Daddy Homer and angel. My sisters, Shubhangi and Sayali, for every laugh and cry we have had together. My brother Mahesh, who gently smiled upon me each time I paused to find the right words.

To my ISHA daughters and sons with whom we danced our first expression of the five elements. To my staff, Alex, Maria, and Blanca,

Supriya, and Jaya, who not only kept my home running and welcoming, but also meticulously took care of every detail regarding my family and me and filled each day and every meal with unconditional love.

And to my heart, my cubs, my daughters, Bhakti and Sharayu, whose love and light inspired this gift to be written for all persons, all daughters, and all sons of the world.

ABOUT THE AUTHOR

Revati "Rani" Puranik is a global business leader and philanthropist on a mission to inspire others to pursue growth and achieve great things. With the personal motto "There's always a way," she strives to help people of all backgrounds find their own path to success and joy.

She is the co-owner, executive vice president, and global CFO of Houston-based Worldwide Oilfield Machine (WOM). The privately held, family-owned oil and gas equipment manufacturing firm has more than four thousand employees and operates in thirteen locations around the world. In addition, Rani chairs the organization's corporate responsibility arm, the Puranik Foundation, a nonprofit that provides educational opportunities for under-resourced children in India at a private residential school, the Vision International Learning Center. In Houston, she chairs Nextgen Innovation Academy, a school slated for grades six through twelve, focused on entrepreneurship, leadership, biotechnology, and sustainable energy.

Widely recognized for her accomplishments and her service, she was named one of the Top 25 Most Influential Women in Energy, serves on the Rice Business Council of Overseers and the World Affairs Council, and is the chair of Next Gen Academies.

As the author of *Seven Letters to My Daughters*, Rani spreads her message of gratitude and shares her philosophy on life: build to give away, grow to give back, lead to listen, stabilize, inspire, and let go. She is a visionary with a two-hundred-year plan as a bridge for the success of future generations.

A free ebook edition
is available with the
purchase of this book.

To claim your free ebook edition:

1. Visit MorganJamesBOGO.com
2. Sign your name CLEARLY in the space
3. Complete the form and submit a photo of the entire copyright page
4. You or your friend can download the ebook to your preferred device

Morgan James
BOGO™

A **FREE** ebook edition is available for you or a friend with the purchase of this print book.

CLEARLY SIGN YOUR NAME ABOVE

Instructions to claim your free ebook edition:
1. Visit MorganJamesBOGO.com
2. Sign your name CLEARLY in the space above
3. Complete the form and submit a photo of this entire page
4. You or your friend can download the ebook to your preferred device

Print & Digital Together Forever.

Snap a photo   Free ebook   Read anywhere

CPSIA information can be obtained
at www.ICGtesting.com
Printed in the USA
JSHW081505030523
41210JS00001B/4